CITYSPOTS
MUN

CW00393406

WHAT'S IN YOUR GUIDEBOOK?

Independent authors Impartial up-to-date information from our travel experts who meticulously source local knowledge.

Experience Thomas Cook's 165 years in the travel industry and guidebook publishing enriches every word with expertise you can trust.

Travel know-how Thomas Cook has thousands of staff working around the globe, all living and breathing travel.

Editors Travel-publishing professionals, pulling everything together to craft a perfect blend of words, pictures, maps and design.

You, the traveller We deliver a practical, no-nonsense approach to information, geared to how you really use it.

CITYSPOTS
MUNICH

Written by Barbara Radcliffe Rogers
Updated by Kate Hairsine

Published by Thomas Cook Publishing
A division of Thomas Cook Tour Operations Limited
Company registration No: 3772199 England
The Thomas Cook Business Park, 9 Coningsby Road
Peterborough PE3 8SB, United Kingdom
Email: books@thomascook.com, Tel: +44 (0)1733 416477
www.thomascookpublishing.com

Produced by The Content Works Ltd
Aston Court, Kingsmead Business Park, Frederick Place
High Wycombe, Bucks HP11 1LA
www.thecontentworks.com

Series design based on an original concept by Studio 183 Limited

ISBN: 978-1-84848-161-9

First edition © 2007 Thomas Cook Publishing
This second edition © 2009 Thomas Cook Publishing
Text © Thomas Cook Publishing
Maps © Thomas Cook Publishing/PCGraphics (UK) Limited
Transport map © Communicarta Limited

Series Editor: Lucy Armstrong
Production/DTP: Steven Collins

Printed and bound in Spain by GraphyCems

Cover photography (Altes Rathaus) © JUPITERIMAGES/Brand X/Alamy

CONTENTS

SYMBOLS KEY

The following symbols are used throughout this book:

ⓐ address **ⓣ** telephone **ⓦ** website address **ⓔ** email
ⓛ opening times **ⓝ** public transport connections

The following symbols are used on the maps:

ⓘ information office		▪	points of interest
✈ airport		O	city
✚ hospital		O	large town
♙ police station		○	small town
🚍 bus station		═	motorway
🚆 railway station		—	main road
Ⓤ U-Bahn		—	minor road
✝ cathedral		—	railway
❶ numbers denote featured cafés & restaurants			

Hotels and restaurants are graded by approximate price as follows:
£ budget price **££** mid-range price **£££** expensive

In addresses, 'Strasse' and '-strasse' (meaning 'street' or 'road')
are abbreviated to 'Str.' and '-str.'

◆ *The twin domes of the Frauenkirche (left) and the lofty Neues Rathaus (right)*

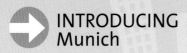

INTRODUCING
Munich

Introduction

The less you know about Munich, the easier it is to define. Right – it's the Oktoberfest city, full of ruddy-cheeked people in lederhosen singing '*Ein prosit, ein prosit*' with foaming steins raised. But after a few trips – or even a few days – you'll soon discover that Munich is more than just beer. There's a dazzling cultural life and a hot music scene for starters.

The quick definition also leaves out the glory of Munich's baroque and rococo churches and the grandeur of its royal palaces. After massive damage in World War II, Munich took a different road from many of its bombed-out counterparts, and instead of constructing a new modern city centre, they rebuilt on the old plan and in much the same style. So the onion-topped domes of Frauenkirche and the Gothic Rathaus tower still stand out over the city rooftops.

It is true that you'll see more traditional dirndls and Tyrolean hats worn in Munich than in other German cities, but in contrast to that and to Bavaria's Catholic conservatism, you'll also meet a different side of Bavaria known as *Liberalitas Bavarica* – Bavarian liberalism. This free-thinking part of the Bavarian psyche comes from its having long been at the crossroads of southern Europe, where the great ancient trade routes crossed the Alps. A little of Italy's *dolce vita* flowed north with the traders and caught on, resulting in an easier, more informal lifestyle and a more jovial nature.

In the end, it's these contradictions and contrasts that make Munich so much fun to visit. It's the classy Max-strasse shops and 21st-century architecture one minute and oompah-pah bands and jingling horse-drawn brewery wagons the next. It's grand opera and Oktoberfest, conservative Catholic farmers and the Glockenbachviertel's gay/lesbian buzz, *haupt* culture and counter-culture. It's Munich, and you'll have a great time there.

◢ *There's more to Munich than a good stein of beer*

When to go

SEASONS & CLIMATE

Oddly, the months when Munich has the most hours of sunshine are also those when it has the most rainfall – May to September. Summer temperatures are rarely uncomfortable, though, so, despite the rain, travel is enjoyable then. In the winter, Munich is frequently snow-covered and often broods under grey skies. But the weather is rarely bitterly cold.

ANNUAL EVENTS

January–February

Fasching Munich's Carnival is celebrated with parties and events held throughout the city. 'Mad Munich', with masked dancers twirling around in the old city centre, takes place on the last three days, ending on Shrove Tuesday.

February–March

Strong beer season Centuries ago German monks brewed a strong beer during Lent to drink for strength while they fasted. The tradition continues with the spring strong beer season.

Late April–early May

Spring festival on the Theresienwiese Lively event held on the Oktoberfest grounds, with music and beer tents.
ⓦ www.muenchner-volksfeste.de
May Dult This event kicks off the Dult year (see Shopping, pages 24–5) with a flea market featuring arts and crafts by Munich artisans, held on the Mariahilfplatz.

Ballet Week This week of performances by the Bavarian State Ballet is held at the National Theatre.
ⓦ www.bayerisches.staatsballett.de

Mid-May
The Long Night of Music An all-night jamfest, city-wide, with places offering everything from jazz to rock, pop, classical and church music. Shuttle buses take visitors to and from venues.
ⓦ www.muenchner.de/musiknacht

Mid-June
Streetlife festival Cars are banned on the Leopold- and Ludwigstrasse boulevards for the weekend, while the street is filled with musicians, dancers and people strolling among kiosks of art, crafts and foods. ⓦ www.streetlife-festival.de

Mid-June–early July
Tollwood summer festival Performances by international musicians and drama groups are held in colourful tents in the Olympic Park. ⓦ www.tollwood.de

Late June
Munich Film Festival The glitz and glittervolk of the film industry converge on Munich to discover new films and talent.
ⓦ www.filmfest-muenchen.de
Munich town run Run 10 km (6 miles) or a half-marathon through some of Munich's neighbourhoods; the Theatinerstrasse, the Hofgarten and the Englischer Garten, ending at Marienplatz.
ⓦ www.sportscheck.com

Late June–early July
Classical music on the Odeonsplatz The Munich Philharmonic Orchestra performs classical music under the stars.

Mid-July
Christopher Street Day (CSD) This event, held during the second weekend of the month, is named after the first public demonstration by gays and lesbians in 1969 on Christopher Street in New York when they protested against discriminatory police raids. A gay pride parade starts the weekend's events. ⓦ www.csdmuenchen.de

Late July–early August
Jacob's Dult The Dult year is in full swing by the summer with the second market of the year.

Mid-September
Streetlife festival A repeat of the June festival.

Late September–early October
Oktoberfest A world-renowned celebration of Munich brewing (see pages 14–15). At noon on the first day, the Lord Mayor of Munich taps the first keg and the drinking and feasting begins. ⓦ www.muenchen-tourist.de

Mid-October
The Long Night of the Museums Ninety museums, art galleries, churches and cultural institutions open their doors for the evening. Shuttle buses take visitors to and from venues. ⓦ www.muenchner.de/museumsnacht

Late October
Kermis Dult The Kermis marks the closing of the Dult year.

Late November–early December
Tollwood winter festival A festive Christmas market and special musical performances are held in tents on the Theresienwiese. A great place to sample foods from around the world. ⓦ www.tollwood.de

December
Christmas markets Munich's Christmas markets are famous all over Europe for their hand-made gifts, decorations, toys and foods, sold amid twinkling lights and evergreen boughs.

PUBLIC HOLIDAYS
New Year's Day 1 Jan
Epiphany 6 Jan
Good Friday 2 Apr 2010, 22 Apr 2011, 6 Apr 2012
Easter Monday 5 Apr 2010, 25 Apr 2011, 9 Apr 2012
Labour Day 1 May
Whit Monday 24 May 2010, 13 June 2011, 28 May 2012
Corpus Christi 3 June 2010, 23 June 2011, 7 June 2012
Feast of the Assumption 15 Aug
German Unity Day 3 Oct
All Saints 1 Nov
Christmas Day 25 Dec
St Stephen's Day 26 Dec

Oktoberfest

Munich is actually the third-ranking city in the world in beer production, but it ranks first in the minds of travellers who flock there each October for the famed Oktoberfest. The roughly six million visitors each year make it the world's biggest folk festival, and although beer may be the central theme to most visitors, the festival includes a lot more.

It all began in October 1810, when King Ludwig I, then a crown prince, married Princess Therese of Saxony-Hildburghausen, and all of Munich was invited to a big wedding party in the fields at the city gates. The fields were renamed Theresienwiese ('Theresa's fields') in her honour, since abbreviated to the 'Wies'n'.

The horse race that closed the festivities was so popular that they decided to repeat it the next year, adding an agricultural fair (still held every third year). Within a few years, some amusements, including a carousel, were added, and stalls and beer stands began to join the festival. In 1896, the first of the big beer tents appeared, and by then a full amusement park was a regular feature.

In order to take better advantage of the September weather, the fest has been moved to begin in mid-September and continue until the first weekend of October. Between the official opening announcement of '*O'zapft is!*' ('It's tapped!'), and the closing '*Aus is!*' two and a half weeks later, the six million visitors drink six million litres of beer and 33,000 litres of wine, while eating 480,000 barbecued chickens, 180,000 pairs of sausages, 560,000 pork knuckles and nearly 100 roasted oxen.

Before the Oktoberfest begins, a parade representing the landlords of the tents and the breweries processes to the Wies'n in decorated carriages, along with the horse-drawn brewery drays, floats and all the beer tent bands. The next day, Sunday, has an even bigger parade with costumed groups representing various regions, riflemen in historical uniforms, the brewery drays and bands, dancers, floats, flag-throwers and other performers.

⬥ *Oktoberfest: the world's biggest folk festival*

History

Munich's story of royal grandeur, war and romance goes back to the Celts, who inhabited the plains of Bavaria until the Romans marched north. The influence of the Romans was not as great as it was elsewhere, and when Germanic tribes arrived from Bohemia, the empire collapsed, and the last Roman legions retreated to Italy in AD 476.

Two centuries later the Romans came back as Christian missionaries, converting Bavaria to Catholicism. Around 788 Benedictine monks helped to establish a small settlement on the banks of the Isar, called München.

In 1158 Frederick Barbarossa, Holy Roman Emperor, issued a decree establishing München (Munich) as an important trade centre. In 1180 the Emperor gave Bavaria to Count Palatine Otto von Wittelsbach, establishing the dynasty that was to survive 738 years – until the end of World War I.

The Wittelsbachs governed well, dividing up the dukedom among family members, then reuniting it over the following centuries. In the 1805 Treaty of Pressburg, Bavaria was declared a kingdom and its duke became Maximilian I Joseph, King of Bavaria. It was his grandson, Ludwig II, who was to carve the most lasting memorials to the family, however. This romantic figure built a string of palaces before he was declared insane and deposed in 1886.

The end of World War I brought the end of the Wittelsbachs, in a revolution led by Kurt Eisner, who was himself deposed, leading to the 'Red Terror' and counter 'White Terror'. The result of this political disruption was Bavaria's incorporation into the

Weimar Republic in 1919. Only four years later, Hitler led his stormtroopers from the beer halls in the abortive Munich Putsch. Bavaria remained a hotbed of Nazism and supported Hitler's rise in 1933. The city suffered heavy devastation from allied bombing during World War II, and by its end lay mostly in rubble. Following the war, Bavaria escaped the division suffered by other parts of Germany, and by the 1950s and 60s had rebuilt its major buildings and regained its reputation as a place of good-natured charm, meanwhile re-establishing its commercial and industrial base.

⬤ *Schloss Neuschwanstein (see page 109), one of Ludwig II's palaces*

Lifestyle

Say you're going to Munich, and everyone immediately pictures you sitting in a beer hall clunking huge foaming steins, singing drinking songs accompanied by a wheezing oompah-pah band. For better or for worse, this is most of the world's image of Bavaria. And they're half right.

Beer, to Bavarians, isn't just an alcoholic drink. It's the water of life, part of their ancient heritage, and drinking it in beer halls and gardens is a vital part of the social experience and community life.

Of course, beer isn't the whole story. Life in Bavaria is about a lot of other things, and social life takes other forms. But for the traveller who wants to feel immediately welcome and part of the local scene, a beer garden is a good place to begin.

Brewing has a long history in Munich. In the late 1500s, Duke Wilhelm V decided that with a court of 700-plus people, it made better sense to brew his own beer than to buy it. So was born the court brewery (*hofbrau*), whose brew was good and cheaper than the imported stuff, making it so popular that larger and larger quarters were needed for a beer hall. The Hofbräuhaus became a local institution, and continued serving beer even after 1944 bombing raids destroyed all but a part of the main beer hall.

The Hofbräuhaus is only one of several beer halls in central Munich – the Augustinerkeller, Altes Hackerhaus and several other beer halls draw crowds daily. In the summer, locals are more likely to move to another time-honoured venue, the beer garden, but few travellers follow them there. They should, because the experience is even more quintessential to the Munich lifestyle and, like the beer halls, they bring together all ages and all classes of people. Some have be-dirndled barmaids, at others you buy your beer inside and carry it to any table, except where you see a *Stammtisch* sign (those are reserved for regulars). The gardens are shaded by big old trees, and the largest of them seat 2,000 people. The last beer is served at 22.00. For two of the best, go to Hirschgarten, near Nymphenburg, and Paulaner Brauhaus, southwest of Sendlinger Tor.

🔺 *Beer gardens are an intrinsic part of Munich's appeal*

Culture

From the first, the Wittelsbachs poured money and enthusiasm into building their city-centre palace, the Residenz. This started an artistic tradition that was continued by some of the greatest baroque architects and artisans, and firmly re-established by a group of Europe's leading early 20th-century painters.

Along with the 16th-century Antiquarium, whose giant vaulted ceiling was frescoed in high Renaissance style, the highlight of the palace, the exquisite rococo Court Theatre, is by court architect François Cuvilliés. Cuvilliés also created the rococo hunting lodge at Nymphenburg, the Amalienburg. The stucco work that decorates the little lodge is by another of the period's great masters, J B Zimmerman.

But the work that is most often cited as the definition of German rococo is the Asamkirche. Marble pillars swirl upwards to support a curving balcony from which hang garlands and festoons of gold flowers. Cherubim form the finials on the confessional, itself richly carved, and silver angels point your attention to the polychrome Virgin in an altar niche. The only other work of the Asam brothers (considered the masters of this style) which compares to this church is at Weltenburg Abbey (see page 116).

A group of revolutionary painters brought the next peak in Munich's artistic reputation, at the same time that a group of equally iconoclastic architects were reshaping Munich's streetscapes with *Jugendstil* (art nouveau). The painters, led by Vassily Kandinsky, first gathered south of Munich in Murnau (see page 105), and included Franz Marc, Gabriela Münter,

The gloriously over-the-top Asamkirche

Paul Klee and Alexej von Jawlensky. It was Marc who named the region the Blue Country, because of the sky and the mountains. Expressionists didn't paint in three dimensions, so colour was everything. The painters relished the great variety in Murnau's ever-changing light.

To these Expressionists, colours represented ideas and characteristics, and not necessarily as they were seen in nature – hence Marc's famous blue horses (blue indicated that they were calm and content). They chose the name *Der Blaue Reiter* (the Blue Riders) in reference to St George; the symbolic Blue Rider is seen in their works slaying the dragon of old ideas and strict academy rules in art.

The group eventually left Murnau to live and paint in Munich. Works by Kandinsky and the other 'Decadent' artists were destroyed by the Nazis, but Gabriela Münter hid her collection of them in the cellar of her home – now the Münter House Museum in Murnau – throughout the Third Reich, and even during the allied occupation. Today, the Lenbachhaus in Munich (see page 95) contains the largest collection of these works anywhere.

From rococo to the Blue Riders, Munich and the nearby art towns of Murnau and Dachau have carved a lasting place in Europe's art heritage.

⊙ *The Englischer Garten: a huge stretch of green in the city centre (see page 76)*

Shopping

Dedicated shoppers can get a high just walking down the streets in central Munich, where shop windows are tempting works of art. Step into the little world of the **Fünf Höfe** (ⓦ www.fuenfhoefe.de) shopping precinct in the old town for the city's smartest venue, the Five Courtyards, where architecture and fashion design join forces. Enter these courtyards through Scheffnerhof, on Weinstrasse, or from Brienner Strasse, behind the Frauenkirche, and you may never leave.

For shopping that leaves the plastic a little more intact, head west into Karlsplatz and descend to the 53 shops and two department stores in the underground shopping mall that runs all the way to the main train station. These downtown stores are open 09.00–20.00 Monday–Saturday.

Less predictable, quirkier and priced for students are the funky mix of small shops in the Maxvorstadt neighbourhood, a short walk north of the centre. Past the Siegestor Arch and University, on Schellingstrasse, Türkenstrasse and adjacent streets are boutiques and shops with affordable clothing. The labels may not be so recognisable, but the clothes are cool.

Back in the old town, not far from the Fünf Höfe, the Schrannenhalle is a 19th-century glass and iron market building that has morphed into the home of more than 50 market and crafts stalls. One-off and original works in a variety of media make good souvenirs and gifts.

Auer Dulten, Southern Germany's most famous flea market, takes place three times a year in the southwest part of the city, around the Mariahilf church. Hundreds of stalls sell new and used merchandise, everything from old clothes to an astonishing selection of porcelain and kitchenware. Dates are around May Day, late July/early August and late October, each fair lasting a full week. ⓐ Rosenheimerplatz ⓘ (089) 233 30 294 ⓦ www.auerdult.de ⓝ Tram: 27; bus: 52

⬤ *Traditional clothing at Loden-Frey (see page 70)*

USEFUL SHOPPING PHRASES

What time do the shops open/close?
Um wieviel Uhr öffnen/schließen die Geschäfte?
Oom veefeel oor erffnen/shleessen dee geshefter?

How much is this?
Wieviel kostet das?
Veefeel kostet das?

Can I try this on?
Kann ich das anprobieren?
Can ikh das anprobeeren?

My size is ...
Ich habe Größe ...
Ikh haber grerser ...

I'll take this one, thank you
Ich nehme das, danke schön
Ikh neymer das, danker shern

This is too large/too small/too expensive
Es ist zu groß/zu klein/zu teuer
Es ist tsu gross/tsu kline/tsu toyer

Although December is not prime tourist season, it is a good time to visit Munich for the holiday festivities and decorations. Shop windows glow and every square seems to harbour a Christmas market with pots of steaming *Glühwein* (hot spiced wine) to warm your hands around. Craft stalls sell gifts and holiday decorations and a general flavour of good cheer and holiday spirit prevails.

The most famous *Christkindlmarkt* takes place in Marienplatz from the first day of Advent until Christmas Eve.

Eating & drinking

Bavarian food ranges from the hearty, meaty and often heavy traditional dishes to the heights of 21st-century world food presented by Munich's star chefs. Most of us want to sample the traditional foods, though, as part of the Bavarian experience – and because they go so well with all the fine beers available here.

Nothing could be more quintessentially Bavarian than a *Bauernschmaus*, a platter-like plate overflowing with roasted pork – some smoked, some fresh – and sausages, accompanied by finely cut sauerkraut and *Semmelknödel*, a tasty dumpling.

Other dishes you'll see on menus are *beinfleisch*, tender boiled beef with horseradish; *Kalbshaxe*, roasted veal shanks; *Kalbsrahmbraten*, veal with cream; *Spanferkel*, roast suckling pig and some of the dishes associated with Vienna – *Wiener schnitzel* and *Schnitzel Holstein*, both delicious veal dishes.

Sausages, called *Wurst*, are common as snacks or lunches; don't even think of going to Regensburg without sampling their delicious local *Bratwurst*, which is at its best from the Wurstkuchl, a tiny kitchen under the Danube bridge. In Munich, the morning snack of choice is *Weisswurst*, a white sausage only eaten before noon, and usually before 11.00. It tends to be eaten

PRICE CATEGORIES
Price ratings in this book are based on the average price of a main dish without drinks.
£ up to €10   ££ €10–20   £££ over €20

USEFUL DINING PHRASES

I would like a table for ... people, please
Ich möchte einen Tisch für ... Personen, bitte
Ish merkhter inen teesh foor ... perzohnen, bitter

Waiter/waitress!
Herr Ober/Frau Kellnerin!
Hair ohber/frow kell-nair-in!

May I have the bill, please?
Die Rechnung, bitte?
Dee rekhnung, bitter?

I am a vegetarian. Does this contain meat?
Ich bin Vegetarier (Vegetarierin fem.). Enthält das hier Fleisch?
Ish bin veggetaareer (veggetaareerin). Enthelt dass heer flyshe?

Where is the toilet, please?
Wo sind die Toiletten, bitte?
Voo zeent dee toletten, bitter?

I would like a cup of/two cups of/another coffee/tea, please
Ich möchte eine Tasse/zwei Tassen/noch eine Tasse
Kaffee/Tee, bitte
*Ikh merkhter iner tasser/tsvy tassen/nok iner tasser
kafey/tey, bitter*

I would like a beer/two beers, please
Ich möchte ein Bier/zwei Biere, bitte
Ikh merkhter ine beer/tsvy beerer, bitter

with a fresh pretzel and a beer.

Vegetarians may worry that the meat-heavy cuisine of Munich will leave them going hungry, but there are veggie options on the menu at even the most traditional Munich restaurants, including the Weisses Brauhaus and the Ratskeller (see pages 74–75).

In terms of beer, although the products of the various breweries differ, Munich's beers fall into four main categories. *Helles* is a light beer, a slightly malty lager. *Dunkel* is dark, a bit like porter, malty, but more caramelised. *Pilsner* is a hoppy pale lager. *Weissbier* is light in colour, but rich in taste, a cloudy beer made from wheat. It is also stronger than the others, and always served in glasses, not steins. A fifth group of beers includes all the seasonals, such as *Maibock* in the spring. You may also hear of the *Radler*, a drink like shandy – half beer and half lemonade.

● *Cheeses, cold meats and pretzels feature heavily in Munich cuisine*

⬥ *Relax over a beer at the Augustinerkeller (see page 74)*

Since most beer halls have large tables to share, you'll almost certainly be expected to *prosit* with locals. Here's the right way to do it: raise your stein and clink it full-on with your companion's, each held straight up vertically. If you're drinking wheat beer, however, tilt it so you clink just the bottom of the glass – that's easy to remember because wheat beer is served in a fluted glass with a thick bottom, so clinking it broadside would be asking for a broken glass.

If you're after something non-alcoholic, a couple of the old-fashioned coffee houses – now getting rarer in Munich – survive on the western side of the city, a genteel reminder of pre-war Europe (see page 99). They serve coffee and cakes by day, cocktails in the evening (often with live music laid on, too) and the occasional light meal.

Entertainment & nightlife

Munich, for all its Bavarian conservatism, rocks after dark, with more than enough noisy beer halls, cool bars and hot sounds. Most of Munich's entertainment venues are on the southern and western sides of the city. For the young and the restless, especially of university age, Schwabing is the place to be. And for alternative lifestyles, the place to be is in the Glockenbachviertel, around Gärtnerplatz. The exact antithesis of the traditional beer hall scene, which hasn't changed much in the last century, Munich's relatively new and thriving gay and lesbian life centres here. Its lively scene is generally an open one, so gay or straight, you're welcome. This, and the artists and musicians who call this neighbourhood home, make the Glockenbachviertel a centre for nightlife and entertainment. By contrast, you'll find downtown Munich has more in the way of beer halls reverberating with '*Ein prosit*' and well-dressed opera-goers than trendy bar-hoppers.

What Munich lacks in clubs, it more than makes up in entertainment venues, where on almost any night of the week you can hear and see performances of everything from grand opera to hard-core rock. No matter how high or low your brow is, you'll find your beat in Munich. The most important music venues are:

Circus Krone

When Faithless came to Munich, they played here, as have all the other stars who've appeared in the city. Whether it's a concert, a musical road show or comedy act – or the circus, whose home it is all winter – this is the Münchners' favourite venue. ⓐ Zirkus-

● Tollwood summer festival at Olympiapark

Krone-Str. 1-6, off Marsstr. ☎ (180) 524 7287 Ⓦ www.circus-krone.de
Ⓝ Tram: 16, 21, 27

Das Deutsche Theater

Broadway and West End shows open their European tours
here, or you may see an international ballet troupe or any
performance that needs a stage. ⓐ Werner-Heisenberg-
Allee 113 ☎ (089) 5523 4444 Ⓦ www.deutsches-theater.de
Ⓝ U-Bahn: Fröttmaning

Staatstheater am Gärtnerplatz

Musicians love this venue for its superb acoustics (jazz-lovers
rejoice at its sparkling sounds) and it's also a stage for opera,
ballet and musical shows. ⓐ Gärtnerplatz 3 ☎ (089) 218 51960
Ⓦ www.staatstheater-am-gaertnerplatz.de Ⓝ U-Bahn:
Frauenhoferstrasse; tram 17, 18; bus: 52, 152

Tollwood

The twice-yearly Tollwood Festival is one of Europe's best
known, featuring top German names and international stars
of pop, rock, jazz and folk music. All the top Bavarian bands
play daily, and a craft show surrounds the performance venues.
☎ 0700 3838 5024 Ⓦ www.tollwood.de Ⓝ Winter: S-Bahn:
Hackerbrücke; U-Bahn: Theresienwiese; tram: 18, 19; bus: 58, 66;
summer: U-Bahn: Olympiazentrum; tram: 20, 21; bus: 36, 41, 43,
81, 86

The Staatstheater am Gärtnerplatz

Sport & relaxation

SPECTATOR SPORTS

Football

If you're more into watching sport than taking part, take in a football match at the 66,000-seater **Allianz Arena** (ⓐ Allianz Arena, Werner-Heisenberg-Allee ⓦ www.allianz-arena.de ⓜ U-Bahn: Fröttmaning) , built for the 2006 World Cup and home to both of Munich's first division clubs: FC Bayern Munich and TSV 1860 Munich. The stadium changes colour depending on which team is playing! For match tickets visit ⓦ www.fcbayern.t-com.de or ⓦ www.tsv1860.de.

PARTICIPATION SPORTS

For all Munich's city chic, its residents like to walk, hike, run, cycle, sail and paddle in their spare time, and they find places for those sports in the city and in the lakes and Alpine slopes nearby. The Englischer Garten is a great place to unwind but, if you're feeling more active, the riverside park's level paths are perfect for cycling, jogging and walking. You can even go rafting on the Isar, with **Flösserei Josef Seitner** (ⓐ Lindenweg 1, Wolfratshausen ⓘ 08171 785 18 ⓜ S-Bahn: Wolfratshausen).

Most watersports enthusiasts head south to the **Starnbergersee** (ⓦ www.sta5.de) for sailing and kayaking. This long glacial lake is ringed by a 64 km (40 mile) walking path. In addition, the König-Ludwig-Weg, a nine-day 123 km (76 mile) walking route that starts at Starnbergersee, connects sites associated with the Bavarian king Ludwig: Berg, Starnberg, Kloster Andechs (Andechs Abbey) and his castle at Neuschwanstein. Luggage transfer is available.

North of Munich, a walking and cycling trail stretches the length of the Danube. To get through the steep-banked Danube Gorge between Weltenburg and Kelheim, you can either cross by boat at Weltenburg and climb over the steep hills that enclose the gorge, or take the boat to Kelheim. Bike tours follow the river from Vienna, in Austria, to the Danube source in the Black Forest.

In Regensburg, a 90-minute train ride away, you can rent bicycles for spins along the river from several shops, including **Bikehaus** (ⓐ Bahnhofstr. 17 ⓦ www.bikeprojekt.de), near the railway station. To explore the river from water level, rent canoes at **Kanu & Outdoor Platzek** (ⓦ www.kanu-outdoor.de) in Niedertraubling, 7 km (4 miles) south of Regensburg.

⬥ Kayaking is popular in the lakes region

Accommodation

Accommodation in Munich and Bavaria covers all tastes and budgets, from 5-star luxury at Helmut Yan's Kempinski Hotel to the friendly vibe of the city's hostels. For those travelling on a budget, look out for a *Gasthof* (inn), *Pension*, or *Zimmer Frei* (bed & breakfast).

Advance booking is wise at almost any time of year, but essential in the summer and around Oktoberfest. Weekends are more likely to be filled during the summer around the lakes, and more available in the city. Online booking services are common for hotels, but many small inns have their own websites where you can book directly too. The **Munich Tourist Office** offers a hotel booking service on their website (ⓦ www.muenchen.de), or contact them directly (see page 136).

HOTELS

Easy Palace Station Hotel £ In the no-traffic zone, very close to the Hauptbahnhof (main train station), the hotel has rooms on several levels, from spacious en-suite rooms to dorms and rooms with shared bath. ⓐ Schützenstr. 7 (The Old Town) ⓣ (089) 552 5210 ⓦ www.easypalace.de ⓝ U-Bahn: Hauptbahnhof

> ### PRICE CATEGORIES
> Average price of a double hotel room, with breakfast.
> **£** up to €100   **££** €100–200   **£££** over €200

Hotel Garni-Flora £–££ Excellent location and the warmth of
a family-owned business make this modest hotel in an historic
building an attractive place to stay. Internet service is available.
ⓐ Karlstr. 49 (Western Munich) ⓣ (089) 597 067 ⓦ www.hotel-
flora.de Ⓝ Tram: 20, 21

Hotel Pension Mona Lisa £–££ The charming family-operated
hotel is in a classy neighbourhood just off Maximilianstrasse
and around the corner from the Englischer Garten. Individually
decorated rooms have en-suite baths, hair dryers, TV, phones and
minibars. ⓐ Robert-Koch-Str. 4 (Eastern Munich) ⓣ (089) 2102 8380
ⓦ www.hotelmonalisa.de Ⓝ Tram: 17

Creatif Hotel Elephant £–£££ A large buffet breakfast is included
in the rates at this hotel near the Hauptbahnhof, where rooms range
from modest to quite luxurious. Parking and airport van service
are available. ⓐ Laemmerstr. 6 (The Old Town) ⓣ (089) 555 785
ⓦ www.creatifelephanthotel.com Ⓝ U-Bahn: Hauptbahnhof

Deutsche Eiche £–£££ This hotel 200 m (219 yards) from the
Viktualienmarkt has been the centre of the gay/lesbian scene
since long before it was out of the closet. Also a meeting place
for artists, musicians and others in Munich's creative community,
the hotel offers stylishly decorated rooms and a central location.
ⓐ Reichenbachstr. 13 (The Old Town) ⓣ (089) 231 1660
ⓦ www.deutsche-eiche.com Ⓝ Tram: 17, 18

Hotel Biederstein £–£££ Bright and airy rooms are close to the
Englischer Garten and Schwabing, and within a short walk of

the major museums. In summer, breakfast is served on the garden terrace, and the staff are helpful in suggesting nearby dining. ⓐ Keferstr. 18 (Eastern Munich) ⓣ (089) 389 9970 ⓦ www.hotelbiederstein.de ⓝ U-Bahn: Münchner Freiheit

Hotel Mark ££ On a quiet side street opposite the Hauptbahnhof and in the midst of sights, shopping, restaurants and entertainment, the hotel is handy for public transport. Rooms are plain, but well equipped, with internet connections and soundproofing. ⓐ Senefelderstr. 12 (The Old Town) ⓣ (089) 559 820 ⓦ www.hotel-mark.de ⓝ U-Bahn/S-Bahn: Hauptbahnhof

⬤ *Helmut Yan's dazzling Kempinski Hotel at the airport*

Hotel Deutsches Theater Stadtmitte ££–£££ A five-minute walk from the Hauptbahnhof, the hotel shares its location with a theatre. Rooms are decorated in the Laura Ashley mode, and have private baths, minibars and hair dryers. Most have internet. ⓐ Schwanthalerstr. 15 (The Old Town) ⓣ (089) 889 9950 ⓦ www.hotel-deutsches-theater.com Ⓝ U-Bahn: Sendlinger Tor

🔺 *Hotel Platzl: smart and central*

Hotel Platzl ££–£££ The location, halfway between Marienplatz and Max-Joseph-Platz, is ideal for sightseeing and access to restaurants, theatre and shopping. Rooms on the back overlooking the Hofbräuhaus can be noisy until midnight, but all rooms are well decorated, the breakfast excellent and the staff very helpful. ⓐ Sparkassenstr. 10 (The Old Town) ⓣ (089) 237 030 ⓦ www.platzl.de ⓤ U-Bahn/S-Bahn: Marienplatz

Hotel Central £££ Attractive rooms and onsite parking are advantages of this small, friendly hotel within sight of the Dachau rail station. Use your Munich Card to commute into the city. ⓐ Münchner Str. 46A, Dachau ⓣ (08131) 5640 ⓦ www.hotel-central-dachau.de

Kempinski Hotel Airport München £££ From the minute you step into the soaring lobby of this 5-star hotel designed by Helmut Yan, filled with full-grown palm trees and banks of flowers, you know your room will be just as stunning – and state-of-the-art. All the luxuries in a clean, user-friendly design, plus a full-service spa. ⓐ Terminalstr. Mitte 20, Munich Airport ⓣ (089) 97820 ⓦ www.kempinski-airport.de ⓢ S-Bahn: Flughafen München

HOSTELS

Easy Palace City Hostel £ A discount on meals at the hostel's own Sinans Restaurant (Italian and Asian foods) is a perk of staying in this friendly hostel with private, family and dorm rooms. Breakfast not included. ⓐ Mozartstr. 4 (Eastern Munich) ⓣ (089) 558 7970 ⓦ www.easypalace.de ⓤ U-Bahn: Goetheplatz; bus: 58

THE BEST OF MUNICH

If you have only a few days to spend in Munich, you can concentrate your attention on the central sights, perhaps spending one day on a tour that includes Ludwig II's fairy-tale castles.

TOP 10 ATTRACTIONS
These are the sights and experiences you won't want to miss in and around Munich.

- **Glockenspiel** The giant animated clock in the tower of the Neues Rathaus performs two or three times daily (see page 61)

- **Residenz Palace** The complex of city palaces where the Wittelsbachs lived and played (see page 66)

- **Nymphenburg** The Wittelsbachs' airy summer palace with its beautiful gardens and park (see page 94)

- **Asamkirche** Over-the-top rococo (see page 90)

- ***Weisswurst* and a pretzel** Be sure to order these before 11.00 (see page 27)

- **Schwabing** Join students, artists, musicians and Munich's young crowd on the city's Left Bank (see pages 46–7 and 81)

- **Beer garden or beer hall** Hoist your stein and sing '*Ein Prosit*' with the locals (see pages 18–19)

- **Haus der Kunst and Lenbachhaus** Munich houses a treasury of 20th-century art, including works of the Blue Riders (see pages 82 and 95)

- **Deutsches Museum** One of the world's best science and tech museums, with lots of hands-on exhibits (see page 82)

- **Day tour to King Ludwig's castles** You have to see Neuschwanstein and Linderhof to believe them (see page 109)

🔽 *The impressive Schloss Nymphenburg*

Suggested itineraries

HALF-DAY: MUNICH IN A HURRY

Begin or end at Marienplatz, to see the Glockenspiel perform.
Look inside Peterskirche and, if it's a clear day, get a good view
from its tower (or from that of the Rathaus). Wander through
the Viktualienmarkt, perhaps stopping for a beer. To the left of
the Rathaus is a street leading to Odeonsplatz, on the way passing
the enormous royal Residenz. Just beyond it is the Hofgarten.
Leave time to visit a beer hall, perhaps the Hofbräuhaus or the
Augustinerkeller, closer to Marienplatz.

1 DAY: TIME TO SEE A LITTLE MORE

After wandering around the Old Town, allowing time for a look
at the rococo Asamkirche, and a stroll down Sendlinger Strasse,
choose one of the royal palaces to tour. The Residenz is so big
you'll need to decide which half to see – morning and afternoon
tours are different. On a nice day, opt for Nymphenburg,
where you get the bonus of the gardens and the pretty little
Amalienburg. Head for Schwabing in the evening for dinner
and the nightlife.

2–3 DAYS: TIME TO SEE MUCH MORE

With a bit more time, you might want to see whichever royal
palace you didn't opt for the first day, and indulge in some of
the fine art museums in Munich. Take a walk in Schwabing to
see the art nouveau houses. Spend an evening sampling the
nightlife of Munich's arty gay/lesbian neighbourhood around
Gärtnerplatz or take in a concert or opera performance. If you

have a third day, spend it touring the palaces of King Ludwig, which you can do on a day tour from Munich.

LONGER: ENJOYING MUNICH TO THE FULL

Push the buttons and ring all the bells at the Deutsches Museum, stroll in the Englischer Garten at least as far as the Chinese Tower – resting over a beer and maybe lunch in their beer garden. Make a pilgrimage to Dachau, but don't limit it to the concentration camp. See the pretty town and its hilltop castle, and if art is your thing, don't miss the civic art museum.

⬤ *The Residenz: hallways lined with pictures*

Something for nothing

Schwabing, the area of Munich where artists and the intelligentsia lived at the turn of the 20th century, was filled with everything new and exciting in those heady years before World War I. Along with the new wave of Expressionist painting which threw out all the old rules came a new wave of architecture and decoration. Known elsewhere as art nouveau, in Germany it was called *Jugendstil* – young style.

Breaking loose from old styles – which by the 1800s had become yet another rework of Gothic or classical – these architects dared to decorate buildings in bright colours, to surround doors and windows with sweeping curves (the reverse or 'whiplash' curve was a favourite), and add floral decoration, asymmetrical forms, unusual textures, fanciful wrought-iron work, even stylised faces.

The houses that line the streets on either side of Leopoldstrasse create a free art gallery, with building after building designed by some of the movement's foremost names. You could spend an entire day on a *Jugendstil* treasure hunt here and not spend a euro.

Begin at the Giselastrasse U-Bahn stop, walking down Martiusstrasse to see three long blocks of *Jugendstil*, especially numbers 1, 3, 5 and 7. Wander in almost any direction from the end of the street, or explore the parallel streets of Trautenwolfstrasse and Ohmstrasse.

After this introduction, cross busy Leopoldstrasse to Franz-Joseph-Strasse. At number 19 is a pharmacy with peacocks between the windows and a curved door frame. The building at the corner of Friedrichstrasse is painted even more brightly than it probably was when built. Continue on to see houses on Elisabethstrasse, looking to the left down Isabellastrasse before following it to the right to Bauernstrasse. A right there takes you across a park to Ainmillerstrasse, and some of the most over-the-top buildings in the neighbourhood, one to the left at Römerstrasse 11 and others at Ainmillerstrasse 20 and 22. By the time you've seen these, you'll be ready for a drink, straight ahead, on Leopoldstrasse!

🔵 *It costs nothing to admire the art nouveau streets of Schwabing*

When it rains

A shopping mall of 130 shops, good restaurants, its own brewery and even its own Christmas market make the recently built **Flughafen München** (Munich Airport ☏ (089) 975 00 ⓦ www.munich-airport.de Ⓢ S-Bahn: Flughafen München) a destination for locals as well as an arrival point for visitors. The fact that shops are open all the time – even on Sunday – means that people come here from the city for a Sunday afternoon shopping spree, or when the weather dampens a planned retail adventure along the city's streets. To encourage this, the policy is that prices will be the same as city-centre or other mall shops, and you'll find that shops do stick to this rule. You can buy everything from a chocolate bar to a Lamborghini here.

A busy international airport may not be the first place you'd look for *Gemütlichkeit*, let alone a microbrewery, but you can make the convivial **Airbräu brewery** (☏ (089) 975 93111 ⓦ www.airbraeu.de), where locals and tourists mingle over a beer and good Bavarian food, your first or last stop in the city, or treat it as locals do – as a destination of its own. At the centre are the huge gleaming copper brewing vats, and a live band often plays. Ask for the brewery's very own Wiesn beer, Jet A1, or take a brewery tour and sample all the varieties.

Between the two knock-out modern terminals is a huge open plaza, where you'll find a beer garden, entertainment and, in December, a full Christmas market. Inside Terminal 2 is a branch of the Hofbräuhaus and beautiful food courts, serving everything from sushi and *pad Thai* to pasta. Playrooms keep children amused, and through the soaring glass atrium of the Kempinski Hotel is a full spa. Use of the pool, fitness room, saunas and steam baths is €18 for two hours or €29 for the day.

◔ *There's more to the airport than arrivals and departures*

On arrival

TIME DIFFERENCE
Like the rest of Germany, Munich is on Central European Time
(CET), an hour ahead of Greenwich Mean Time (GMT) in winter
and British Summer Time (late Mar–end Oct).

ARRIVING
By air
Flughafen München (Munich International Airport, see page 48),
is among Germany's largest airports – and certainly its newest
and most modern. It is served by the German national airline,
Lufthansa, and dozens of others, including easyJet. Its two state-
of-the-art terminals are well equipped and service is so efficient
that it has Europe's best record for fast and accurate delivery of

● *International trains arrive at the Hauptbahnhof*

baggage, as well as its fastest flight transfer time (30 minutes). S-Bahn line S8 is the best line to take to and from the city centre, although S1 also connects from both the Marienplatz and Hauptbahnhof stations, with transfers taking around 35 minutes.

By rail

International trains arriving from all parts of Europe, as well as those from most other parts of Germany, come into Munich's Hauptbahnhof, the central train station. Near Karlsplatz, the station is a short walk from the major sights of the old city centre, and is also the central hub for transport; almost all the U-Bahn and S-Bahn lines stop there. Trains from eastern points often arrive at Ostbahnhof, which is further from the centre, but also connected by most major transit lines.

By road

The Hauptbahnhof is also the arrival and departure point for long-distance **Eurolines** coaches (operated in Germany by Deutsche Touring, ⓐ Hirtenstr. 14 ⓣ (089) 8898 9513 ⓦ www.eurolines.com). You'll find their bays and gates just to the west of the station.

If you are thinking of driving in Munich, the best advice is: don't. Instead, park outside of the Green Zone (*Umweltzone*) and enjoy Munich's excellent public transport service. The *Umweltzone* has been introduced in the inner city to reduce particulate pollution. Only motorists with low-emission cars and an *Umweltplakette* (Emission Sticker) are allowed to drive in this zone, or risk a fine of €40. It is possible to purchase the sticker online (assuming your car is eligible) from abroad for €14.99 including VAT and postage. For details consult ⓦ www.tuev-sued.de or ⓣ (089) 579 10.

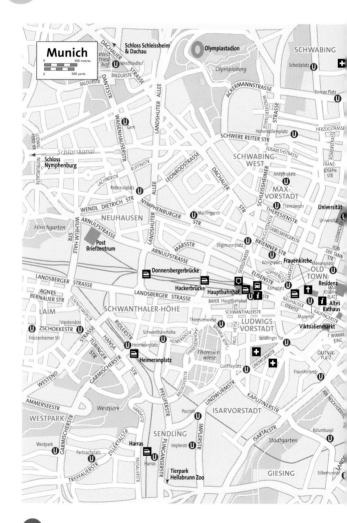

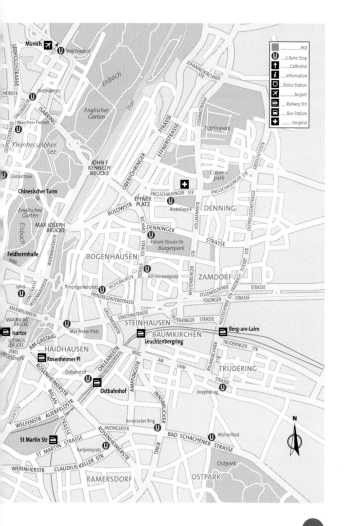

FINDING YOUR FEET

Munich is a very easy city to navigate, either on foot or by public transport. Many of the major attractions are within the 'ring' – a series of streets that circle the old town, roughly following the path of the old city walls. Much of the area within that ring is pedestrianised. Pick up a free map of the city (including the U-Bahn and S-Bahn) in the tourist information offices at the airport, Hauptbahnhof or in the Rathaus on Marienplatz. This is also the place to get any transit passes or a Welcome Card (see opposite).

ORIENTATION

Marienplatz is the heart of Munich – geographically and practically. Most main transit lines connect there, it's where the Rathaus (town hall) is, and many of the major sights are within a five-minute walk. Kaufingerstrasse, which becomes Neuhauser Strasse, is a wide pedestrian street that leads west to another hub, Karlsplatz. Just beyond is the Hauptbahnhof. To the east of Marienplatz, past the Isartor, is the River Isar, and across it are the neighbourhoods of Haidhausen and Bogenhausen. North of Marienplatz, behind the impressive Rathaus, is Max-Joseph-Platz, where the former royal residence is located, and beyond it is Odeonsplatz. Ludwigstrasse continues north, turning into Leopoldstrasse as it enters the student quarter of Schwabing. East of Schwabing is the vast *Englischer Garten* (English Garden), which extends almost to the river. South of Marienplatz is the Viktualienmarkt, a large market square, and beyond it lies Gärtnerplatz, an arty neighbourhood that is home to the city's gay/lesbian community.

IF YOU GET LOST, TRY ...

Excuse me, do you speak English?
Entschuldigen Sie, sprechen Sie Englisch?
Entshooldigen zee, shprekhen zee eng-lish?

**Excuse me, is this the right way to the old town/
the tourist office/the station/the bus station?**
Entschuldigung, geht es hier zur Altstadt/zur
Touristeninformation/zum Bahnhof/zum Busbahnhof?
*Entshooldigoong, gayt es here tsoor altshtat/zur
touristeninformatsion/tsoom baanhof/tsoom busbaanhof?*

Can you point to it on my map, please?
Können Sie es mir bitte auf der Karte zeigen?
Kernen see es meer bitter owf der kaarte tsygen?

GETTING AROUND
Public transport

Munich's excellent U-Bahn (serving the inner city) and S-Bahn
(serving the suburbs) systems, run by MVV, are easy to use, with
stations and entrances well marked and signage easy to follow
even if you don't speak German. There's also a network of trams
which run from early morning until around 01.00.

Several money-saving ticket schemes are available, including
the one- or three-day Welcome Card for unlimited transport and
discounted admission to museums and attractions. Better value

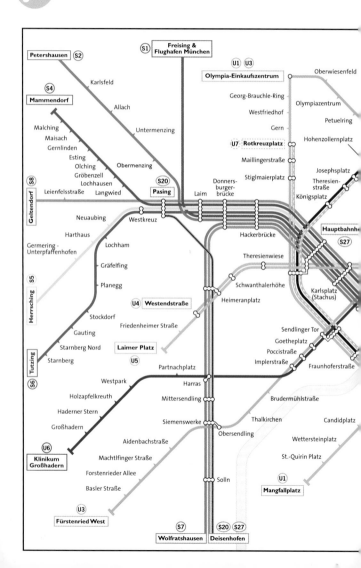

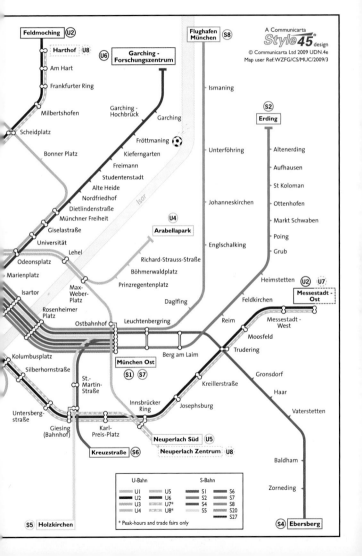

might be a travel card, also available as a Partner Card good for up to five people travelling together. If you don't expect to use public transport often on any single day, a strip of ten tickets for €11 would be the best buy. For further information on public transport, including buses, visit the MVV website Ⓦ www.mvv-muenchen.de

Taxis

It is not easy to hail a taxi, but the free Munich map (available from the local tourist offices, see page 136) shows the location of taxi ranks throughout the city. Hotels and restaurants will always summon a taxi for you, too.

Outside Munich

Getting around Bavaria is easy, even if you choose not to hire a car. The Munich S-Bahn connects the city to both Starnbergersee and Ammersee in the lakes region. Frequent trains to Regensburg, 90 minutes away, connect to towns along the Danube.

Car hire

All the major car hire companies are represented in the airport and within the city. It is wise to book your vehicle ahead to be sure of availability. Remember that Germans drive on the right.

Avis ⓐ Nymphenburger Str. 61 ⓣ (089) 1260 0020 Ⓦ www.avis.com
Budget ⓐ Landsberger Str. 18 ⓣ (089) 5022 2752 Ⓦ www.budget.com
Hertz ⓐ Bahnhofsplatz 2 ⓣ (089) 5502 256 Ⓦ www.hertz.com

Ⓞ *Marienplatz is the hub of the city*

THE CITY OF
Munich

The Old Town

Marienplatz is a lively plaza in the heart of Munich's old town, with the wonderfully Gothic façade of the Altes Rathaus forming one entire side. Streets radiate from it in a web, leading to Peterskirche, the Viktualienmarkt and the Fünf Höfe shops (see page 24). The wide main shopping street, Kaufingerstrasse (which does in fact mean, literally, 'shopping street'), leads to Karlsplatz. To the north of Marienplatz is the regal Max-Joseph-Platz, bounded by the royal palace (Residenz) of the Wittelsbach dynasty, whose seven-century benevolent rule of Bavaria shaped the Munich we see today.

SIGHTS & ATTRACTIONS

Altes Rathaus (Old Town Hall)

Almost enclosing one end of Marienplatz is a typically Bavarian building from the 1400s, the old town hall, which once formed one of the gates of the old city wall. You have to admire Altes Rathaus from the outside as the building isn't open to the public. ⓐ Marienplatz 15 ⓝ U-Bahn/S-Bahn: Marienplatz; tram: 19

Feldherrnhalle (Field Marshal's Hall)

An almost exact copy of a loggia in Florence, Italy, the open gallery holds statues honouring 19th-century German military leaders. During the Third Reich, Hitler added a memorial to those killed in his failed *putsch*, which was stopped just beside this building. He ordered that anyone passing it must salute the guards who were permanently stationed in front of it, to which

Munich residents protested by cutting through Viscardigasse, the alley behind the Feldherrnhalle, which soon became known as the 'dodger's alley'. The Nazi memorial was removed in 1945. ⓐ Odeonsplatz ⓣ (089) 290 671 ⓦ www.schloesser.bayern.de ⓝ U-Bahn/S-Bahn: Odeonsplatz/Marienplatz

Frauenkirche (Cathedral of Our Lady)

The two onion-shaped domes on their matching square towers have become a symbol of Munich. Begun in 1468, the cathedral was completed – except for the towers – 20 years later. The towers were added a few decades later. Near the door is the elaborate tomb of Emperor Ludwig the Bavarian, a bit florid for the otherwise spare lines of the church's interior. ⓐ Frauenplatz 1 ⓛ 10.00–17.00, lift up the south tower open 10.00–17.00 Mon–Fri, Apr–Oct ⓝ U-Bahn/S-Bahn: Marienplatz; tram: 19

Glockenspiel

High in the Neues Rathaus central tower is perhaps Munich's most popular attraction, as you can tell by the hundreds of people who gather in Marienplatz for its several daily performances. The upper figures (which are larger than life-sized) show the wedding of a 16th-century duke, complete with a tournament during which one of the riders is knocked off his horse. Below, costumed members of the coopers' guild (barrelmakers) dance in thanksgiving for the end of the plague. ⓐ Marienplatz ⓛ 11.00, 12.00, 17.00 Mar–Oct; 11.00 Nov–Feb ⓝ U-Bahn/S-Bahn: Marienplatz; tram: 19

Hofbräuhaus

Though locals are rarely seen there, the Hofbräuhaus has become

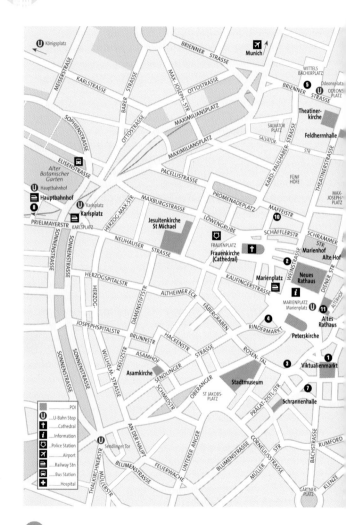

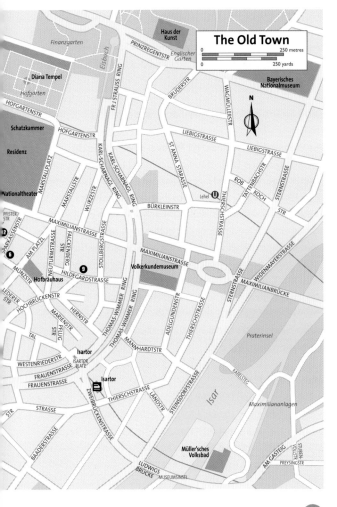

a rite of passage, not to mention a meeting place, for tourists. The brewery is much older than the 1897 building, dating from the 16th century. Oompah bands perform nightly, swaying singers surround the long tables and the barmaids perform athletic feats by carrying astonishing numbers of filled steins. Am Platzl 9 (089) 2901 3610 www.hofbraeuhaus.de 09.00–00.00 U-Bahn/S-Bahn: Marienplatz; tram: 19

Jesuitenkirche St Michael (St Michael's Jesuit Church)

The Renaissance-to-baroque church was begun in 1583, and its vault is Europe's second largest (only St Peter's in Rome is larger). Sculptures and paintings add to its grandeur, which was meticulously restored after the church was severely damaged by bombing in November 1944. In the crypt, entered from the right of the main altar, is the *Gruft*, a landmark on the King Ludwig trail. Some, not all, of the Wittelsbach dynasty are here, including Ludwig II, in a casket rather less grandiose than that of Ludwig I in the Frauenkirche. Neuhauser Str. 52 (089) 231 7060 www.st-michael-muenchen.de *Gruft* 09.30–16.30 Mon–Fri, 09.30–14.30 Sat U-Bahn/S-Bahn: Marienplatz; tram: 19. Admission charge (*Gruft*)

Max-Joseph-Platz

Rather more grand than the intimate Marienplatz, this is a proper square, defined by the façades of the Wittelsbach Residenz and the Nationaltheater. In the centre is a statue of Bavaria's Maximilian I, who had hoped to be portrayed on horseback. Locals are fond of saying that he is beckoning a waiter from the café opposite, but the king himself quipped privately that

⬤ *The neo-Gothic façade of the Neues Rathaus*

it looked as though he were on the loo. U-Bahn: Odeonsplatz; tram: 19

Neues Rathaus (New Town Hall)

The elegant new town hall is replete with enough delicate Gothic pinnacles and stonecarving to fool most into thinking it dates from that period. In reality, it dates from the late 1800s, when neo-Gothic was the rage. Part way up its 85 m (279 ft) tower is the famous Glockenspiel (see page 61) and at the very top is the Münchner Kindl, the little monk that is the city's symbol. From the tower is a 360° view of Munich. ⓐ Marienplatz ⓣ (089) 2332 3191 ⓛ 10.00–19.00 May–Oct & during Christmas markets, 10.00–17.00 Mon–Fri, Nov–Apr ⓝ U-Bahn/S-Bahn: Marienplatz; tram: 19

Peterskirche (St Peter's Church)

Carved in 1492 by master carver Erasmus Grasser, St Peter in his bishop's mitre surveys from the high altar the other masterpieces of religious art gathered in Munich's oldest church. You can admire most of Munich from the tower of this church, after a heart-pumping climb. ⓐ Rindermarkt 1 ⓣ (089) 260 4828 ⓦ www.erzbistum-muenchen.de/StPeterMuenchen ⓛ 09.00–18.30 Mon–Fri, 10.00–18.30 Sat & Sun, summer; 09.00–17.30 Mon–Fri, 10.00–17.30 Sat & Sun, winter ⓝ U-Bahn/S-Bahn: Marienplatz. Admission charge

Residenz

The eight buildings that make up the palace complex began in the 1300s, continuing through to the 1826 addition of the Königsbau by King Ludwig I. The grandest room is the 16th-century Antiquarium with its impressive gallery. During World War II, a bomb dropped squarely in its centre, and you can see that the floor changes 21 squares from the far end, where it was replaced. Today the buildings house several museums, including the Schatzkammer (treasury) where the state jewels are displayed (see page 69). The small room with Chinese tapestries is where the hearts of the royal family members were removed at their death, to be buried separately. Adjoining the Grottenhof, with its fountain built to resemble a grotto, is the Hall of Vengeance, completely covered in scenes from the legends of the Nibelungs. After severe damage in World War II, the Residenz was meticulously restored, with Americans loaning the money for its restoration. Note that

⬤ *The Viktualienmarkt*

morning and afternoon tours are different, so you need both to see the whole palace. **a** Max-Joseph-Platz 3 **t** (089) 290 671 **w** www.residenz-muenchen.de **L** 09.00–18.00 summer; 09.00–17.00 winter **N** U-Bahn: Odeonsplatz; tram: 19; bus: 53. Admission charge

Viktualienmarkt

The city's oldest food market is still its most popular gathering place, and you'll mingle here with housewives at their morning shopping, young professionals grabbing lunch or an after-work beer and just about everyone else in Munich. Its aisles are spacious and all is clean and tidy. **L** Usually 08.00–18.00 Mon–Sat **N** U-Bahn/S-Bahn: Marienplatz; bus: 52

CULTURE

Nationaltheater

The 1823 Opera House was destroyed in World War II, but, unlike most such buildings, it has kept its original decorative detail and chandeliers. The Nazis did not allow anything to be taken from buildings to protect them from destruction during the war but a still-unidentified official in the Ministry of Culture photographed the entire interior and spirited its decorative objects away into hiding. The rebuilt Opera House opened in 1963. It is one of Europe's finest, a thoroughly modern venue with near-perfect acoustics and visibility, but with the look of the traditional European theatre. It is known for its dramatic new stagings of German operas. **a** Max-Joseph-Platz 2 **t** (089) 2185 1920 **w** www.bayerische.staatsoper.de **L** Ticket office: 10.00–19.00

THE REST OF THE WITTELSBACHS

The romantic story of Ludwig II gets so much press that it's easy to lose sight of the remarkable dynasty that ruled Bavaria from 1180 until 1918 – an unusually long time. Despite the grandiose living style seen in their in-town palace, the Residenz, the Wittelsbachs were modest kings with far less pomp and ceremony than other European royalty of the time. They were well liked and are still widely admired. Their descendants still live in Bavaria, and during the Nazi era they worked against Hitler and were imprisoned in concentration camps.

Mon–Sat or one hour before performance starts Ⓝ U-Bahn: Odeonsplatz/Marienplatz; tram: 19

Schatzkammer (Treasury)

The crown of Henry II (1230–80) and other Wittelsbach treasures are set in eye-level cases. Most precious of all is the bejewelled figure of St George, slaying an enamelled dragon set with emeralds. Beneath the knight's visor is hidden a perfect miniature face.
ⓐ Max-Joseph-Platz 3 ⓣ (089) 290 671 Ⓦ www.residenz-muenchen.de Ⓛ 09.00–18.00 summer; 09.00–17.00 winter
Ⓝ U-Bahn: Odeonsplatz; tram: 19; bus: 53. Admission charge

Stadtmuseum

Think of this as a whole set of different museums under one roof, covering local history, arts and culture. Puppets get especially good coverage, with regular performances and an entire section of their own. German silent films from the collections are shown daily, and you can get a greater appreciation for the city you see today after a look at the photographs of it in 1944. ⓐ St-Jakobs-Platz 1 ⓣ (089) 2332 2370 ⓦ www.stadtmuseum-online.de ⓛ 10.00–18.00 Tues–Sun ⓝ U-Bahn: Marienplatz/Sendlinger Tor. Admission charge

RETAIL THERAPY

Galeria Kaufhof The large downtown department store Kaufhof covers five floors with arty displays of clothing, household goods and more. ⓐ Marienplatz ⓣ (089) 231 851 ⓦ www.galeria-kaufhof.de ⓛ 09.00–20.00 Mon–Sat ⓝ U-Bahn/S-Bahn: Marienplatz

Hemmerle If your taste in baubles runs towards those worn by the Wittelsbach princesses, head for the shop that made its name as the court jeweller. One-off and limited-edition jewellery by the best Bavarian designers. ⓐ Maximilianstr. 14 ⓣ (089) 242 2600 ⓦ www.hemmerle.de ⓛ 12.00–18.00 Mon, 10.00–18.00 Tues–Fri, 10.00–17.00 Sat ⓝ U-Bahn/S-Bahn: Marienplatz

Hugendubel English-language books and travel guides and maps will interest the traveller at Munich's biggest bookshop. ⓐ Marienplatz 22 ⓣ (01801) 484 484 ⓦ www.hugendubel.de ⓛ 09.30–20.00 Mon–Sat ⓝ U-Bahn/S-Bahn: Marienplatz

Loden-Frey The best-known name in fine woollen coats and

hats designed for Alpine winters, Loden-Frey also sells men's, women's and children's clothing in more contemporary styles.
ⓐ Maffeistr. 7 ⓣ (089) 210 390 ⓦ www.loden-frey.com
ⓛ 10.00–20.00 Mon–Sat ⓜ U-Bahn/S-Bahn: Marienplatz

Ludwig Beck am Rathauseck The place to go for necessities, but with a good section of Bavarian handiwork and crafts, Ludwig Beck has another unexpected bonus. On the top floor is Germany's best selection of CDs of hard-to-find classical works and operas.
ⓐ Marienplatz 11 ⓣ (089) 236 910 ⓦ www.ludwigbeck.com
ⓛ 10.00–20.00 Mon–Sat ⓜ U-Bahn/S-Bahn: Marienplatz

▲ *Max Krug: souvenirs aplenty*

Max Krug When you really just need a souvenir of Bavaria, whether it's a pewter-topped beer stein or a hand-carved nutcracker, you'll find it in this well-known shop. They have been in business nearly a century. ⓐ Neuhauser Str. 2 ⓣ (089) 224 501 ⓦ www.max-krug.com ⓛ 09.30–20.00 Mon–Sat ⓝ U-Bahn/S-Bahn: Marienplatz

Servus Heimat From T-shirts with a slick print of a pretzel to gnome baking trays, this brightly coloured store is the perfect place for a kitsch but cool present for those back home. ⓐ St-Jakobs-Platz 1 (in the Stadtmuseum) ⓣ (089) 2370 2380 ⓦ www.servusheimat.de ⓛ 10.00–20.00 Tues–Sat, 10.00–18.00 Sun ⓝ U-Bahn: Marienplatz/Sendlinger Tor

TAKING A BREAK

Biergarten am Viktualienmarkt £ ❶ No trip to Munich is complete without a morning break for juicy hot *weisswurst*, pretzels and beer, and there's no more pleasant place than under the honey locust blooms at the edge of the market. ⓐ Viktualienmarkt ⓛ 09.00–22.00 Mon–Sat ⓝ U-Bahn/S-Bahn: Marienplatz

Bohne und Malz £ ❷ Hidden away from the inner-city bustle just behind Marienplatz, this cafe with its tasteful wooden interior is great for a coffee break, snack or a quick meal. ⓐ Weinstr. 3 ⓣ (089) 295 202 ⓦ www.bohneundmalz.de ⓛ 09.00–01.00 Mon–Sat, 12.00–22.00 Sun, summer; 09.00–00.00 Mon–Sat, winter ⓛ U-Bahn: Marienplatz

Café Frischhut £ ❸ Pop into this traditional haunt of the people who work in the nearby Viktualienmarkt for the *Schmalznudel*, a deep-fried sweet doughnut. ⓐ Prälat-Zistl-Str. 8 ❶ (089) 268 237 ❶ 05.00–17.00 Mon–Sat Ⓝ U-Bahn/S-Bahn: Marienplatz

Café Glockenspiel £ ❹ Arrive early if you hope for a window table for the city's best view of the famed Rathaus clock's performances. But the coffee is good any time, and the pastries are, too. ⓐ Marienplatz 28, 5th floor ❶ (089) 264 256 Ⓦ www.cafe-glockenspiel.de ❶ 10.00–01.00 Mon–Sat, 10.00–19.00 Sun Ⓝ U-Bahn/S-Bahn: Marienplatz

Café Luitpold £ ❺ Old-timers who remember pre-war Munich get misty-eyed over the sumptuous surroundings that were, but the rebuilt café still basks in the glory of the greats who sipped their coffee there including Johann Strauss and Kandinsky. ⓐ Brienner Str. 11 ❶ (089) 242 8750 Ⓦ www.cafe-luitpold.de ❶ 09.00–20.00 Mon–Fri, 08.00–19.00 Sat Ⓝ U-Bahn: Odeonsplatz

Hofpfisterei £ ❻ This traditional bakery sells amazingly tasty organic wholegrain breads and cake, as well as sandwiches and coffee. ⓐ Sparkassenstr. 12 ❶ (089) 293 595 Ⓦ www.hofpfisterei.de ❶ 07.30–18.30 Mon–Fri, 07.30–13.00 Sat Ⓝ U-Bahn/S-Bahn: Marienplatz

Wirsthaus zum Straubinger £–££ ❼ Midday is the most crowded time at this noisy tavern serving hearty Bavarian comfort food including *bauernschmaus*, a farmer's plate heaped with a sampling

of sausages and meats with dumplings and sauerkraut.
ⓐ Blumenstr. 5 ⓣ (089) 232 3830 ⓦ www.zumstraubinger.de
ⓛ 10.00–01.00 Mon–Sat, 11.00–23.00 Sun ⓝ U-Bahn/S-Bahn:
Marienplatz

AFTER DARK

RESTAURANTS

Augustinerkeller £–££ ❽ Bavarian food and atmosphere rule at
this centrally located beer cellar and restaurant, where servings
are prodigious and the food some of the best of its kind in the
city. ⓐ Arnulfstr. 52 ⓣ (089) 594 393 ⓦ www.augustinerkeller.de
ⓛ 10.00–01.00 ⓝ U-Bahn/S-Bahn: Hauptbahnhof

Conviva im Blauen Haus £–££ ❾ Emphasis on fresh and tasty
food that creatively mixes the flavours of northern Italy, Austria
and Bavaria with lunch menus for under €10. Housed in a former
workshop of the Kammerspiel Haus, this slick café and restaurant
is part of a training project for disabled people. ⓐ Hildegardstr. 1
ⓣ (089) 2333 6977 ⓦ www.convivamuenchen.de ⓛ 11.00–01.00
Mon–Sat, 18.00–01.00 Sun ⓝ U-Bahn/S-Bahn: Marienplatz

Weisses Brauhaus £–££ ❿ An old brewery for Bavaria's famed
wheat beer has morphed into a traditional restaurant that
locals rave about. Enjoy hearty portions of the old standard
Wurst, *Knödel* (dumplings) and farmers' platters plus lake fish
and a few vegetarian options. ⓐ Tal 7 ⓣ (089) 290 1380
ⓦ www.weisses-brauhaus.de ⓛ 08.00–01.00 ⓝ U-Bahn/
S-Bahn: Marienplatz; tram: 19

Ratskeller ££ ⓫ Traditionally these restaurants in the basements of the town hall were gathering places for the townspeople, and they have morphed into some of the most authentically German of all eating places. All the old favourites are on the menu along with a few surprises (a couple of vegetarian options, for example). ⓐ Marienplatz 8 ⓣ (089) 219 9890 ⓦ www.ratskeller.com ⓛ 10.00–00.00 ⓝ U-Bahn/S-Bahn: Marienplatz

Pfistermühle ££–£££ ⓬ Small dining rooms, attentive service and a top-rate chef combine to make this one of Munich's best choices for sampling updated Bavarian specialities. ⓐ Pfisterstr. 4 ⓣ (089) 2370 3865 ⓦ www.platzl.de ⓛ 12.00–23.00 Mon–Sat ⓝ U-Bahn/S-Bahn: Marienplatz; tram: 19

BARS & CLUBS

Atomic Café Nightclub with live acts and concerts, a bar and a disco with a big range of beats. Check out the Klangbild on their website for what music's playing when. ⓐ Neuturmstr. 5 ⓣ (089) 228 3054 ⓦ www.atomic-cafe.de ⓛ 22.00–03.00 Tues–Thur, 22.00–04.00 Fri & Sat (opens an hour earlier for concerts) ⓝ U-Bahn/S-Bahn: Marienplatz; tram: 19

Master's Home Popular as one of the best singles bars in Munich, this eccentrically decorated place – all wood panelling, leather club chairs and a peculiar assortment of colonial bric-a-brac – is also an Italian restaurant of some note. ⓐ Frauenstr. 11 ⓣ (089) 229 909 ⓦ www.mastershome-muenchen.de ⓛ 18.00–00.00 ⓝ S-Bahn: Isartor

Eastern Munich

To the east of the old centre, beyond Isartor, the River Isar is bordered by a swathe of greenery well used by locals for walking, cycling and sunbathing. To the north is the even larger greensward of the Englischer Garten, Europe's largest urban park. Bordering the park is Munich's liveliest neighbourhood, Schwabing, where artists, musicians, students and younger travellers congregate.

SIGHTS & ATTRACTIONS

Englischer Garten (English Garden)

Benjamin Thompson, an American who made himself indispensable to the Wittelsbachs in the late 1700s by revamping their army, creating social welfare systems and improving agriculture, designed these gardens to reclaim a marshy area alongside the river. The Chinesischer Turm (Chinese Tower), modelled after one in Kew Gardens, was built in 1789–90. Today it is a magnet for the young and thirsty, on account of the beer garden that spreads below it. Also in the gardens are a Japanese garden and teahouse, various monuments and another beer garden (with an older clientele) at Seehaus, overlooking the Kleinhesseloher See, a lake inside the gardens. ⓐ Prinzregentenstr. ⓣ (089) 224 319 ⓦ www.schloesser.bayern.de ⓛ Sunrise to sunset ⓝ U-Bahn: Universität/Münchner Freiheit; bus: 54, 154

Hofgarten

The old royal court gardens began in the 1600s, and although they are laid out quite formally, they avoid the just-so stuffiness

◢ *The Chinesischer Turm*

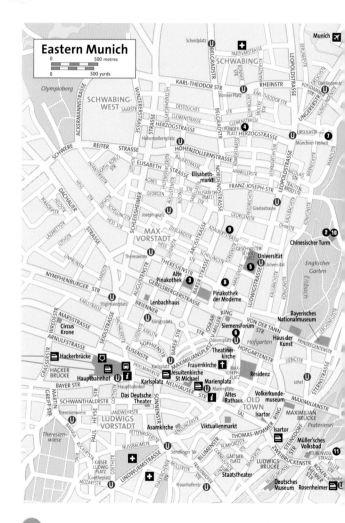

Eastern Munich

0   500 metres
0   500 yards

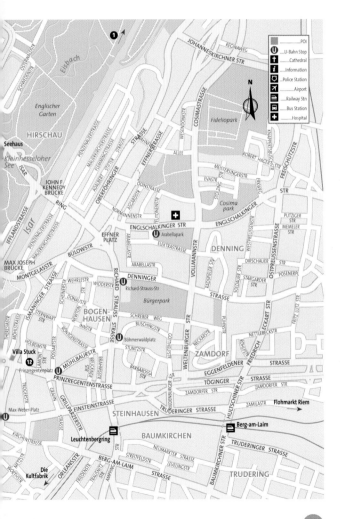

of many and are a nice place to relax, with flowers, fountains and the yellow towers of the Theatinerkirche as a backdrop. Odeonsplatz www.schloesser.bayern.de U-Bahn: Odeonsplatz; tram: 19; bus: 53

Isar

The river cuts a swathe through the city, which Munich has wisely kept bordered in parks, so you can walk or bike for miles along it. Roadway and foot bridges cross it frequently and museums stand on its islands. Between two of these, just east of the city centre, a dam provides a man-made waterfall. S-Bahn: Isartor; tram: 17, 18, 20

Isartor

Dating from the 1300s, Isartor is the oldest of the three remaining city gates from the days of the salt traders. These merchants stopped at inns along the Tal, the street that runs from the river into Marienplatz. S-Bahn: Isartor; tram: 17, 18, 20

Müller'sches Volksbad

If you want a slice of local life, as well as a look at one of Munich's most outstanding *Jugendstil* (art nouveau) buildings, take your swimsuit to the magnificent public bath beside the Isar. Built from 1897 to 1901 and freshly restored to its original splendour, the bath offers swimming, steam baths and a café where you can eat an inexpensive meal. Rosenheimer Str. 1 (01801) 796 223 Pool: 07.30–23.00; sauna: 09.00–23.00 (women only all day Tues & Fri until 15.00) S-Bahn: Isartor; tram: 18

Schwabing

It's Munich's Left Bank, where university students blend with artists, free-thinkers and progressives to create a buzz that you can feel in the air. It begins at the arch on Ludwigstrasse, spilling out into the surrounding streets. Tree-lined Leopoldstrasse continues on from Ludwigstrasse, with a continuous line of cafés, nightspots and shops. The neighbourhood was the centre of the Modernist movement in Germany, and was the home of Thomas Mann, Kandinsky and other luminaries of the era.

CULTURE

Alte Pinakothek

The history of European art through the 1700s is traced here through more than 800 paintings, each a major representative piece. The Venetian school, for example, is represented by Titian and Tiepolo, and the museum holds one of the world's major collections of the works of Peter Paul Rubens. ⓐ Barer Str. 27 ⓣ (089) 052 16 ⓦ www.pinakothek.de/alte-pinakothek ⓛ 10.00–20.00 Tues, 10.00–18.00 Wed–Sat ⓝ U-Bahn: Königsplatz; tram: 27; bus: 53. Admission charge

Bayerisches Nationalmuseum (Bavarian Museum)

The art and culture shown in this huge museum is more of the folklife variety than fine arts, although both are represented. Local traditional crafts are a major part of the collections, as are costumes, furnished rooms and decorative arts from the various periods through to early 20th-century art nouveau. ⓐ Prinzregentenstr. 3 ⓣ (089) 211 2401 ⓦ www.bayerisches-

nationalmuseum.de ● 10.00–17.00 Tues, Wed, Fri–Sun,
10.00–20.00 Thur ● U-Bahn: Lehel; tram: 17; bus: 100.
Admission charge (free Sun and holidays)

Deutsches Museum

If you itch to poke at the exhibits and play with the toys in most
museums, look no further. Here you're welcome to do just that,
with interactive exhibits and a plethora of things that light up,
move and make noise. From early sailboats to space probes, the
history of the human love affair with technology is all laid out in
one of the world's foremost science museums. ● Museumsinsel 1
● (089) 21791 ● www.deutsches-museum.de ● 09.00–17.00
● U-Bahn: Fraunhoferstrasse; S-Bahn: Isartor; tram 17, 18.
Admission charge

Haus der Kunst (House of Art)

With typical German stick-it-to-him, Munich turned Hitler's
new museum into a showplace of the very artists and styles
that the dictator ordered burned as decadent. The emphasis
here is on exhibitions and events, so check the website or at the
tourist office to see what's on. ● Prinzregentenstr. 1, West Wing
● (089) 2112 7113 ● www.hausderkunst.de ● 10.00–20.00 Fri–Wed,
10.00–22.00 Thur ● U-Bahn: Lehel; bus 53. Admission charge

Pinakothek der Moderne

For those who prefer the new masters to the old, the Moderne
is the best choice: it is one of the largest museums of 20th-
and 21st-century art in the world, so big that it needs to be split
into four groups. One covers fine arts and new media, one is for

applied arts and design, while the architecture and graphics collections are shown in changing exhibitions. ⓐ Barer Str. 40 ⓘ (089) 2380 5360 ⓦ www.museum-der-moderne.de ⓛ 10.00–18.00 Tues, Wed, Fri–Sun; 10.00–20.00 Thur ⓝ U-Bahn: Königsplatz; tram: 27; bus: 53. Admission charge

⬢ *The Deutsches Museum*

SiemensForum

Enter the high-tech world of cutting-edge science and virtual reality. Communications is the main focus, but other realms of technology are explored, including energy and transport, with lots of opportunity to be hands-on. ⓐ Oskar-von-Miller-Ring 20 ⓣ (089) 6363 2660 ⓛ 09.00–17.00 Mon–Fri ⓝ U-Bahn: Odeonsplatz; bus: 53

Villa Stuck

The only one of Munich's many *Jugendstil* villas which is open to the public, Villa Stuck was the home and atelier of artist Franz von Stuck. The house and garden are filled with Stuck's own work and his extensive art collections. ⓐ Prinzregentenstr. 60 ⓣ (089) 4555 510 ⓦ www.villastuck.de ⓛ 11.00–18.00 Tues–Sun ⓝ U-Bahn: Max-Weber-Platz/Prinzregentenplatz; tram: 18. Admission charge

Volkerkundemuseum (Ethnology Museum)

Most of what's in this cabinet of curiosities has little to do with either Bavaria or even Europe, but it's fascinating anyway, and good for a rainy afternoon. ⓐ Maximilianstr. 42 ⓣ (089) 2101 36100 ⓛ 09.30–17.30 Tues–Sun ⓝ U-Bahn: Lehel; S-Bahn: Isartor; tram: 17, 19

RETAIL THERAPY

Elisabethmarkt Like the Viktualienmarkt, this street market is filled with stalls selling cheese, wine, herbs, bread, sausages and ready-to-eat foods. Stalls have various opening times: the fresh fruit and vegetable growers and butchers tend to open around 08.00 and close at 18.00; other stalls are open by 10.00 and close at 19.00. ⓐ Elisabethstr. at Nordendstr. Ⓝ U-Bahn: Josephsplatz; tram: 27

Flohmarkt Riem (Riem Fleamarket) This is where the locals take their Loden coats and last year's dirndls, along with everything else from CDs to fishing rods. Shopping here requires stamina, but do make your way through the new imports at the outer edges to find the jumble booths in the middle. Prices can be phenomenally cheap. ⓐ Messestadt Ⓦ www.flohmarkt-riem.com Ⓛ 06.00–16.00 Sat (not every Sat in winter, so check website for dates) Ⓝ U-Bahn: Messestadt

Kunst Oase Gilded picture frames that look as though they might have been pinched from Nymphenburg Palace, authentic art nouveau chairs and smaller decorative baubles of various vintages fill every corner. ⓐ Hohenzollernstr. 58 Ⓣ (089) 396 875 Ⓦ www.kunstoase.com Ⓛ 09.00–19.30 Mon–Fri, 09.00–18.00 Sat Ⓝ U-Bahn: Hohenzollernplatz

Words'Worth English-language and art books are the main interests for tourists here, and you'll find plenty of each at this bookshop and its nearby branch. There's even a tiny National Trust shop in a corner among the books. ⓐ Schellingstr. 3 Ⓣ (089) 280 9141 Ⓛ 09.00–20.00 Mon–Fri, 10.00–16.00 Sat Ⓝ U-Bahn: Universität

TAKING A BREAK

Aumeister £ ❶ A pleasant beer garden surrounded by the
green space of the Englischer Garten. ⓐ Sondermeierstr. 1
ⓣ (089) 325 224 ⓦ www.aumeister.de ⓛ 09.00–23.00 Tues–Sun
Ⓝ U-Bahn: Studentenstadt

Biergarten am Chinesischen Turm £ ❷ A young crowd favours
this beer garden in the Englischer Garten, under the Chinese
Tower. ⓐ Englischer Garten 3 ⓣ (089) 3838 730 ⓛ 10.00–00.00
Ⓝ U-Bahn: Giselastrasse

Brasserie Tresznjewski £ ❸ Lunches here are so cheap
that it's a favourite for students from the nearby university.
ⓐ Theresienstr. 72 ⓣ (089) 282 349 ⓛ 08.00–01.00 Sun–Thur,
08.00–02.00 Fri & Sat Ⓝ U-Bahn: Theresienstrasse

Friesische Teestube £ ❹ This cosy tea house offers more than
150 types of tea accompanied by scrumptious cakes. For those
wanting more, there are antipasti, toasties and cheese platters.
Probably the friendliest and quietest cafe in Munich. ⓐ Pündter
Platz 2 ⓣ (089) 348 519 ⓦ www.friesische-teestube.de
ⓛ 10.00–23.00 Ⓝ U-Bahn: Bonner Platz; tram: 12

Ludwig-Maximilian University Cafeteria £ ❺ OK, so it's not
a gourmet palace, but the food is dependable, plentiful and
cheap. Cash only. ⓐ Geschwister-Scholl-Platz 1 ⓛ Lunch only
Ⓝ U-Bahn: Universität

Tambosi – Hofgartencafe £ ❻ A Viennese-style cafe with comfortable armchairs and high ceilings for winter days, and a great terrace for sunny afternoons. Music lovers should check out the Opera-Thursdays (winter only), where music students sing arias between every course of the set menu. ⓐ Odeonsplatz 16 ❶ (089) 298 322 Ⓦ www.thementeam.de ❶ 07.30–01.00 ❶ U-Bahn: Odeonsplatz

AFTER DARK

RESTAURANTS

Bobolovsky £ ❼ There's nothing formal about the pub-like interior of this Schwabing standby, but the food is good and available all day, from full English breakfasts through to midnight noshes. Weekday lunch specials are a bargain at under €6. ⓐ Ursulastr. 10 ❶ (089) 397 363 Ⓦ www.bobolovsky.de ❶ 09.00–01.00 Sun–Thur, 09.00–03.00 Fri & Sat ❶ U-Bahn: Münchner Freiheit

Cohen's £–££ ❽ Despite its modern setting, this homely Jewish restaurant manages to evoke the days before World War II. You don't have to be Jewish to feel its nostalgia – or enjoy its traditional foods, from chopped liver to borscht and burly plates of boiled meats. On Fridays you can hear live *klezmer*. ⓐ Theresienstr. 31 ❶ (089) 280 9545 Ⓦ www.cohens.de ❶ 18.00–00.30 ❶ U-Bahn: Odeonsplatz

Max Emanuel Brauerei £–££ ❾ Popular at lunch with students and artists who like good beer and good *Wurst*. The beer garden (which is closed in winter) is secluded and far more intimate than most in Schwabing. Live Latin music, salsa lessons and the large dance floor are also a draw. ⓐ Adalbertstr. 33 ⓣ (089) 271 5158 ⓦ www.max-emanuel-brauerei.de ⓛ 11.00–01.00 Apr–Oct (beer garden closes at 23.000); 17.00–01.00 Nov–Mar ⓝ U-Bahn: Universität

ChineseTurm Restaurant ££ ⑩ The menu is eclectic, with a few Bavarian specialities. The location is a favourite in the summer, when tables on the terrace overlook the busy beer garden under the Chinese Tower. ⓐ Englischer Garten 3 ⓣ (089) 3838 7327 ⓦ www.chinaturm.de. ⓛ 10.00–23.00 ⓝ U-Bahn: Giselastrasse

Nektar ££–£££ ⑪ Bubble-shaped chairs, comfy pillows on sofa-like benches, changing light colours, this place is on the far edge. Don't worry, though, once you've been there they remember you – or their handprint scan does, and it gets you to the head of the queue. Booking is essential for dinner, especially on weekends. ⓐ Stubenvollstr. 1 ⓣ (089) 4591 1311 ⓦ www.nektar.de ⓛ From 19.00 Tues–Sun ⓝ S-Bahn: Rosenheimer

Käfer-Schenke £££ ⑫ In a careful balance between the finest Bavarian traditions and new culinary concepts and glam, Käfer manages to keep everyone agreeing that it's one of Munich's best. ⓐ Prinzregentenstr. 73 ⓣ (089) 4168 247 ⓦ www.feinkost-kaefer.de ⓛ 11.30–23.00 Mon–Sat ⓝ U-Bahn: Prinzregentenplatz

BARS & CLUBS

Nightlife outside the centre is divided between Schwabing, where students and the arts community congregate, and south of the

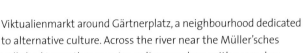

Viktualienmarkt around Gärtnerplatz, a neighbourhood dedicated to alternative culture. Across the river near the Müller'sches Volksbad is another counter-culture enclave, with a number of gay and lesbian bars.

Disco Crash Club nights and disco keep this place just off Leopoldstrasse going until all hours, especially at weekends. ⓐ Ainmillerstr. 10 ⓣ (089) 39 16 40 ⓦ www.discothek-crash.de ⓛ 20.00–01.00 Thur, 21.00–04.00 Fri & Sat Ⓝ U-Bahn: Giselastrasse

Inge's Karotte Lesbian bar south of the Viktualienmarkt. ⓐ Baaderstr. 13 ⓣ (089) 201 0669 ⓦ www.inges-karotte.de ⓛ 18.00–01.00 Mon–Sat, 16.00–01.00 Sun Ⓝ S-Bahn: Isartor

Jazzclub Unterfahrt Every night brings a different artist, and there's a Sunday jam with local musicians. ⓐ Einsteinstr. 44 ⓣ (089) 448 2794 ⓦ www.unterfahrt.de ⓛ 19.30–01.00 Ⓝ U-Bahn: Max-Weber-Platz; tram: 15, 18, 19

Die Kultfabrik With over 20 clubs, bars, pubs, stages and a concert hall, Kultfabrik is a whole entertainment neighbourhood under one roof. ⓐ Grafinger Str. 6 ⓦ www.kultfabrik.de ⓛ Check website for details Ⓝ U-Bahn/S-Bahn: Ostbahnhof

Rote Sonne Chilled club located in a historical arched cellar. Great retro styling and a tasty snack-bar for midnight munchers. ⓐ Maximiliansplatz 5 ⓣ (089) 5526 3330 ⓦ www.rote-sonne.com ⓛ 23.00–late Thur–Sat (check website for weekday opening as it is variable) Ⓝ U-Bahn: Karlsplatz (Stachus)/Odeonsplatz

Western Munich

The area west of the old city centre is not as well known to most travellers as the central and northeastern parts of the city. This may be because its clusters of activity are so widely scattered. The alternative nightlife in the sassy streets around Gärtnerplatz, the open-air sights around Tierpark, the dazzling palaces at Nymphenburg and Schloss Schleissheim, the former Olympic park and the Oktoberfest grounds are not exactly within a short stroll of each other.

SIGHTS & ATTRACTIONS

Asamkirche (Asam church)

You may hear German visitors murmuring '*Tsu fiel*' – too much – as they stand in this small church that is often cited as the very definition of rococo (see page 20). Even the interior marble was selected for its high-contrast swirling patterns. Legend has it that the rough stone at either side of the door is a reference to the Danube cliffs, where the boat of the church's patrons, the Asam brothers, was nearly wrecked, but artists see there the stone 'sketches' for fountains that were never finished because of the death of the sculptor brother, Egin Asam. ⓐ Sendlinger Str. 61–62 ⓣ (089) 260 9171 ⓛ 08.00–17.30 Ⓤ U-Bahn: Sendlinger Tor; bus: 31, 56

Bavaria Filmstadt

Hollywood-on-the-Isar is the nickname for this backstairs look at the Bavarian cinema industry. Stunt shows and the original sets for several German film classics (including *Das Boot*) make

this an entertaining tour. ⓐ Bavariafilmplatz 7, Geiselgasteig
ⓣ (089) 6499 2000 ⓦ www.filmstadt.de ⓛ 09.00–16.00
summer; 10.00–15.00 winter ⓝ Tram: 25. Admission charge

Olympiapark

The grounds of the 1972 summer Olympics are one of Munich's
favourite playgrounds, punctuated by the 290-m (950-ft) tower
that now holds observation decks and a restaurant. Around it
are walking paths, a lake with boats and several buildings which
are landmarks of modern architecture. ⓣ (089) 3067 2414
ⓦ www.olympiapark-muenchen.de ⓛ Olympiaturm (tower):
09.00–00.00; Olympiastadion: 08.30–20.30 summer;

⬤ *The Olympiapark with the huge Olympiaturm*

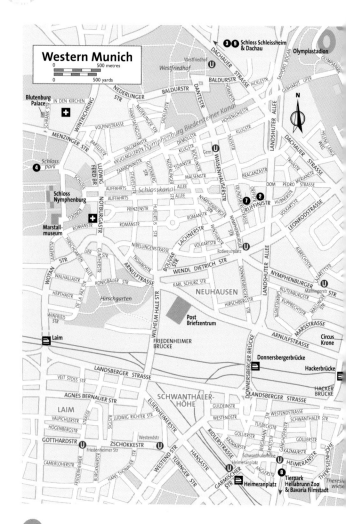

Western Munich

0   500 metres
0   500 yards

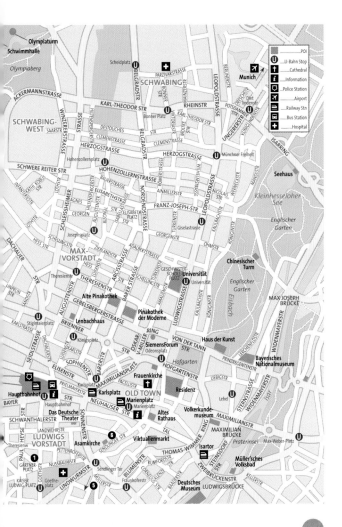

09.00–16.00 winter; see website for tour times U-Bahn: Olympiazentrum. Admission charge for tower and tours

Schloss Nymphenburg (Nymphenburg Palace)

One of the most beautiful of all the Wittelsbach palaces, the summer palace at Nymphenburg is light, bright and liveable, with large windows overlooking the lawns and gardens. Along with the rooms of the palace, also open to the public are the former stables, housing the coach collections of the Marstallmuseum (see page 95). The grounds include beautiful gardens, with pools, pavilions, follies and the graceful little rococo Amalienburg Palace. ⓐ Schlosspark (Eingang 19) ⓣ (089) 179 080 ⓦ www.schloesser.bayern.de ⓛ 09.00–18.00 summer; 10.00–16.00 winter ⓝ U-Bahn: Rotkreuzplatz; tram: 12, 16: Romanplatz; bus: 51; tram: 17. Admission charge

Schloss Schleissheim (Schleissheim Palace)

The complex of baroque palaces includes both the old and new Schleissheim and the Lustheim Palace, set in landscaped gardens. The palaces are sumptuously decorated, and also contain major works of decorative arts and paintings. ⓐ Neues Schloss, Altes Schloss and Schloss Lustheim ⓣ (089) 315 8720 ⓦ www.schloesser-schleissheim.de ⓛ 09.00–18.00 Tues–Sun, summer; 10.00–16.00 Tues–Sun, winter ⓝ S-Bahn: Oberschleissheim; bus: 292. Admission charge

Tierpark Hellabrunn Zoo

More than 5,000 animals of nearly 500 species live along the banks of the Isar, in a zoo whose claim to fame is its success in breeding endangered species. Special areas for children include baby animals, a petting zoo, tours and programmes designed to introduce youngsters to animals. ⓐ Tierparkstr. 30 ⓣ (089) 625 080 ⓦ www.tierpark-hellabrunn.de ⓛ 10.00–22.00 Tues–Sun ⓝ U-Bahn: Thalkirchen; bus: 52. Admission charge

CULTURE

Lenbachhaus

Here, in one setting, is the finest collection of the works of the Blue Riders group, a movement that included Jawlensky, Kandinsky, Klee, Marc and Münter (see pages 20–22). ⓐ Luisenstr. 33 ⓣ (089) 233 32 000 ⓦ www.lenbachhaus.de ⓛ 10.00–18.00 Tues–Sun ⓝ U-Bahn: Königsplatz; tram: 20, 21, 27. Admission charge

Marstallmuseum

Located in the former stables of Nymphenburg Palace, the museum contains a collection of royal coaches that include over-the-top coronation coaches as well as the only-slightly-less-grand everyday vehicles of the royal family. ⓐ Nymphenburgerstr. ⓣ (089) 179 080 ⓦ www.schloesser.bayern.de ⓛ 09.00–18.00 summer; 10.00–16.00 winter ⓝ U-Bahn: Rotkreuzplatz; tram: 12. Admission charge

RETAIL THERAPY

Artefakt One-of-a-kind clothing, contemporary crafts and outstanding gold jewellery by young designers. ⓐ Hans-Sachs-Str. 13, off Müllerstr. ⓣ (089) 260 3108 ⓦ www.artefakt-

DACHAU'S FORGOTTEN LEGACY

The Dukes of Wittelsbach chose the commanding height at the Munich suburb of Dachau to build their summer palace Schloss Dachau, and the town grew first on the hilltop, then spilling down the slopes into the river valley below. The castle's walled gardens with views of Munich's skyline date from 1400, though their present baroque form came later.

In the late 19th century, Dachau became one of Bavaria's 'art towns' where groups of painters gathered in colonies to paint the landscapes. In 1908 they opened a gallery to which the artists all donated paintings, the basis of the outstanding civic art museum's collection. World War I and the economic crash that followed put an end to the art colony, and during World War II the concentration camp took over Dachau's reputation. The Galerien art museum, a few steps from the castle, has a remarkable collection of the works of these *plein air* artists. ⓐ Konrad-Adenauer-Str. 3 ⓘ (08131) 567 516 ⓦ www.dachauer-galerien-museen.de ⓛ 11.00–17.00 Tues–Fri, 13.00–17.00 Sat & Sun ⓝ S-Bahn: Dachau; bus: 720, 722

DACHAU: KZ GEDENKSTÄTTE (CONCENTRATION CAMP)

The camp at Dachau opened in 1933, just three months after Hitler took power, to hold opposition leaders and others whom the new government feared. It was built to house 6,000, but 32,000 were liberated here; today 800,000 people a year come to see the memorial site.

One in five prisoners was Jewish, and although the records were burned by the SS, a total of 210,000 are thought to have passed through. A labour camp rather than an extermination camp, its prisoners produced war materials in Munich factories. Reconstructed dormitories and many original buildings tell the grim story. ⓐ Alte Römerstr., Dachau ⓣ (08131) 669 970 ⓦ www.kz-gedenkstaette-dachau.de ⓛ 09.00–17.00 Tues–Sun ⓝ S-Bahn: Dachau, then bus 724 or 726 from station to KZ Gedenkstätte

⬥ The concentration camp at Dachau: a sobering sight

muenchen.de 🕐 11.00–19.00 Mon–Fri, 11.00–15.00 Sat
Ⓝ U-Bahn: Fraunhoferstrasse

Galerie für Angewandte Kunst München Paintings, sculpture
and crafts in various media are sold in this state-run gallery
that was established in the 1800s to promote Bavarian artists.
Prices begin low enough to make art accessible to all budgets.
ⓐ Pacellistr. 6–8 ☏ (089) 290 1470 🕐 10.00–18.00 Mon–Sat
Ⓝ U-Bahn: Karlsplatz

Konen Six floors of fashion, divided between designer
boutiques and mixed stock. Labels include the likes of Armani,
Guess, Hugo Boss and Polo Ralph Lauren. ⓐ Sendlinger Str. 3
☏ (089) 244 4220 🖥 www.konen.de 🕐 10.00–20.00 Mon–Sat
Ⓝ U-Bahn: Sendlinger Tor

Saturn Just west of Hauptbahnhof is a techie's seventh heaven,
with the latest in electronics: computers, sound systems,
cameras and all their accessories. ⓐ Schwanthaler Str. 115
☏ (089) 510 850 🖥 www.saturn.de 🕐 10.00–20.00 Mon–Sat
Ⓝ U-Bahn: Theresienwiese

Stierblut Terribly cool men's and women's clothing store that
stocks young and funky designers' gear. Expensive but great
for one-off quirky fashion, and commendably friendly staff.
ⓐ Sendlinger Str. 35 & 37 ☏ (089) 2308 7386 🕐 10.00–20.00
Mon–Sat Ⓝ U-Bahn: Sendlinger Tor

TAKING A BREAK

Café am Beethovenplatz £ ❶ Although it's also a full restaurant, the main appeal of this venerable spot is as an old-school coffee house. Jazz or classical music accompanies Sunday brunch. ⓐ Hotel Mariandl, Goethestr. 51 ⓣ (089) 5529 1053 ⓦ www.mariandl.com ⓛ 09.00–00.00 ⓝ U-Bahn: Goetheplatz

Café Ruffini £ ❷ Here's an unusual café; it serves natural foods, free of preservatives and organically grown. Baked goods are made in house. ⓐ Orffstr. 22–24, Neuhausen ⓣ (089) 161 160 ⓦ www.ruffini.de ⓛ 10.00–00.00 Tues–Sun ⓝ U-Bahn: Rotkreuzplatz

Dachau – Café Teufelhart £ ❸ Just a few minutes walk from the Galerien art museum and Schloss Dachau, this bakery with an attached café and an outdoor terrace has good cakes and sandwiches, plus live music most evenings. ⓐ Augsburgerstr. 8 ⓣ (08131) 71133 ⓦ www.dachau-online.de/teufelhart ⓛ 07.30–23.00 Mon & Tues, 07.30–01.00 Wed & Thur, 07.30–02.00 Fri & Sat, 07.30–18.00 Sun ⓝ S-Bahn: Dachau; bus: 720, 722

Schlosscafe im Palmenhaus £ ❹ Stop for coffee and cakes or beer and a meal in the glasshouse of Nymphenburg Palace, where prices are surprisingly non-palatial. Cash only. ⓐ Gardens of Schloss Nymphenburg near entrance 43 ⓣ (089) 175 309 ⓦ www.palmenhaus.de ⓛ 09.30–18.30 Apr–Oct; 09.30–18.30 Tues–Sun, Nov–Mar ⓝ U-Bahn: Rotkreuzplatz; tram 12, 16: Romanplatz; bus: 51, tram 17

AFTER DARK

RESTAURANTS

Makassar £–££ ❺ For spicier food than you're likely to find in the beer halls, head to this Caribbean oasis and sip rum drinks with your Creole dishes. ⓐ Dreimuhlenstr. 25 ❶ (089) 776 959 ⓦ www.makassar.de ⏱ 18.30–01.00 Mon–Sat Ⓝ S-Bahn: Poccistrasse

Altes Hackerhaus ££ ❻ The brewery was there in the 16th century, and although the brewing is now done elsewhere, the same old conviviality remains, along with the litre steins of Hacker-Pschorr and the burly platters of *wursts* and meats with sauerkraut. A speciality is roast suckling pig. ⓐ Sendlinger Str. 14 ❶ (089) 260 5026 ⓦ www.hackerhaus.de ⏱ 10.00–00.00 Ⓝ U-Bahn: Marienplatz/Sendlinger Tor

Big Easy ££ ❼ New Orleans jazz and Cajun cooking might not be what you're expecting in Bavaria, but this is a refreshing place to go when the oompah and *wurst-and-kraut* get on your nerves. ⓐ Frundsbergstr. 46 ❶ (089) 1589 0253 ⓦ www.thebigeasy.de ⏱ 17.00–01.00 Mon–Sat, 10.00–01.00 Sun Ⓝ U-Bahn: Rotkreuzplatz

Estate Menterschwaige ££ ❽ On the banks of the Isar near Tierpark, this historic house, built in the 11th century, has little rooms indoors and courtyard dining in the summer, with sophisticated dishes that update the traditional standbys and add eclectic flavours. The beer garden has a good playground for kids. ⓐ Menterschwaigstr. 4 ❶ (089) 640 732 ⓦ www.menterschwaige.de ⏱ 11.00–00.00 Ⓝ Tram: 15, 25

Schloss Dachau ££ ❾ Popular for afternoon coffee and cakes, but less well known for dinner, the restaurant inside the impressive castle is Dachau's best. The chef lives up to the menu's promise, with braised lamb shanks, veal goulash, roast duck and delicious surprises such as carrot-apricot cream soup with baby shrimps.

⬤ *Dine outside at the Altes Hackerhaus*

ⓐ Schloss Str. 2, Dachau ⓣ (08131) 4543 660 ⓦ www.cafe-restaurant-
schloss-dachau.de ⓛ 10.00–late Wed–Sat, 09.00–late Sun
ⓝ S-Bahn: Dachau; bus: 720, 722

CLUBS & BARS

Milchbar With its giant dance floor, pumping sounds and dim
red lighting, this is a place to party and make new chums, rather
than chill out in a corner. ⓐ Sonnenstr. 12 ⓣ (089) 4502 8818
ⓦ www.milchundbar.de ⓛ 22.00–late Mon, Tues, Thur–Sat
ⓝ S-Bahn: Hauptbahnhof

Mylord For all the gay hangouts, lesbian clubs are a rarity in
Munich; this is it. ⓐ Ickstattstr. 2A, off Müllerstr. ⓣ (089) 2604 498
ⓛ 18.00–21.00 Tues–Thur, 18.00–03.00 Fri–Sun ⓝ U-Bahn:
Fraunhoferstrasse

ⓞ *Cruise boats at Passau*

Land of Lakes

The landscape southwest of Munich is studded with glacial
lakes before it rises to the snowcapped summits of the Alps.
The two largest of these lakes, Starnbergersee and Ammersee,
are also the closest to Munich. Farther south is the Staffelsee,
in the 'Blue Country' made famous by the Blue Rider painters.

GETTING THERE

Starnbergersee and Ammersee are linked to the city by S-Bahn,
and the 70-km (45-mile) drive to Murnau takes under an hour.
Berg is under half an hour from Munich by car.

SIGHTS & ATTRACTIONS

Berg

At the northern end of Starnbergersee, Berg is best known as
the place where King Ludwig II drowned in 1886. A trail from the
village leads to a memorial chapel in the woods above the shore.

Bernried

On the southwest shore of the lake, Bernried is a less busy option
which you can reach by boat from the train station in Starnberg.
The lakeside path here passes the monastery, Klosterweise, whose
elaborate church is open to visitors, as is the nearby Hofmark
church, surrounded by its churchyard. North along the lake and
reached by boat or by the walking path is the Buchheim Museum
(see page 110).

Murnau

At the edge of the largest protected moorland in Europe, Murnau is overlooked by the Zugspitze, a craggy Alp which you can ascend by train and cable car. The unusually luminous atmosphere – a combination of light from the snow-covered mountains and the low, open moorlands – attracted a group of young painters, led by Wassily Kandinsky. These Expressionists, who arrived in 1908, called themselves *Der Blaue Reiter* (the Blue Riders), and this land the Blue Land. Murnau is filled with art that predates the Blue Riders, and with buildings painted in soft pastels and decorated with the lively frescos for which lower Bavaria is known. Fanciful dragons – the symbol of the town's patron saint – adorn the Rathaus and other public spaces. Sometimes St George is also depicted.

🔺 *Possenhofen Palace (see page 108)*

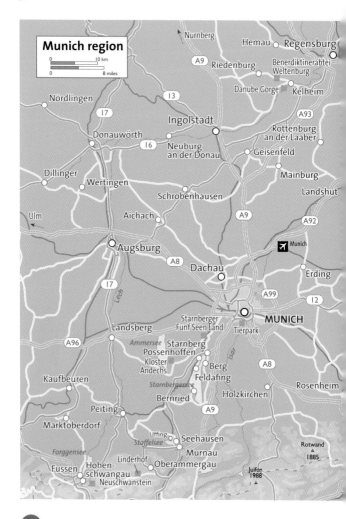

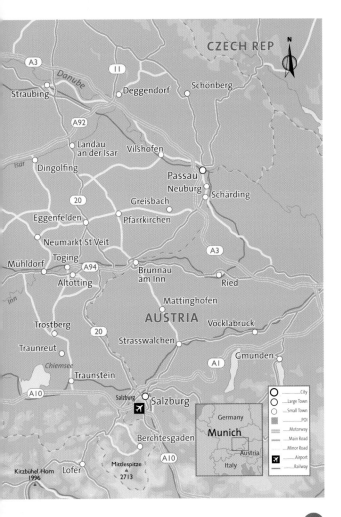

Schloss Possenhofen (Possenhofen Palace)

This imposing yellow palace was built by the father of Elisabeth of Austria. Sisi herself lived here each summer until she left Bavaria to marry Emperor Franz Joseph. The Wittelsbachs arrived by train at the sweet little station here, where the Royal Saloon is now an intimate Sisi museum with a good collection of memorabilia, open only on summer weekends. The castle was restored in the 1950s. It is now in private hands and the interior is not open to visitors.

A little boat can take you to Rose Island, close to the shore, where Sisi and her cousin Ludwig, whose castle was just across the lake in Berg, used to meet in the Italianate villa.

Staffelsee

Smaller than the lakes to the north, Staffelsee has an intimate charm of its own, best appreciated on a walk or cycle around the 22 km (14 mile) *Rundweg*, a path encircling the lake, or from a kayak, which can be hired in Uffing, at the northern shore. You can hire bicycles and electric boats here too, or board a little boat for a circle tour or to travel to Murnau, at the opposite end. Much of the round-lake path goes through nature reserves.

Starnberg

Locals will tell you that the richest people in Germany live here, in this resort town 30 minutes by S-Bahn from Munich. From its tree-lined shore promenade you can see the Alps across the lake. No industry mars the shores or surrounding landscapes, thanks to King Ludwig II. This visionary argued that people would want to come here to enjoy nature, so he banned industrial development. The town is filled with beautiful villas built at the turn of the

20th century, some of which have become inns. The boats which circle the lake and connect the towns around it leave from the dock right at the S-Bahn station, so connecting to hotels anywhere along the lake is easy.

Starnbergersee

Lake Starnberg is a glacial lake, 21 km (13 miles) long, 130 m (427 ft) deep, and a favourite playground for Munich residents. A popular

FURTHER AFIELD TO LUDWIG'S CASTLES

Southwest of Munich, almost at the Austrian border, are two of King Ludwig II's most romantic castles, the fairy-tale Neuschwanstein and the dreamy little 'hunting lodge' of Linderhof. The easiest way to see these from Munich is on a day tour which combines visits to both. They are not far from Murnau, so those visiting the Staffelsee area by car will find them even easier to reach. The towers of Neuschwanstein are a familiar image of Bavaria, set against the snow-covered Alps, but to many, the smaller Linderhof is the lovelier of the two, with its jewel-box rooms, beautiful gardens and elegant fountains.

Schloss Neuschwanstein ☎ (08362) 939 880
🌐 www.neuschwanstein.com 🕐 09.00–18.00 Apr–Sept; 10.00–16.00 Oct–Mar. Admission charge
Schloss Linderhof ☎ (08822) 92030 🌐 www.linderhof.de
🕐 09.00–18.00 Apr–Sept; 10.00–16.00 Oct–Mar. Admission charge

trip is the walk around the lake on a 54 km (34 mile) path. The tourist office can arrange for a tour that includes luggage transfer to your hotel. The popular König Ludwig Weg is a combination of walking paths and boat travel to sites associated with him: Berg, Starnberg, Andechs Abbey and Neuschwanstein; an appropriate way to see these, since he loved walking and hiking.

CULTURE

Buchheim Museum

Lothar-Günther Buchheim, best known as the author of *Das Boot*, but also a collector and an artist of some talent, has housed his collections in a museum of fantasy and imagination.

BAVARIA'S BELOVED SISI

Ludwig may be Bavaria's 'Fairy-Tale King', but it is his cousin Sisi who has captured the hearts of Bavarians as their enduring fairy-tale princess. Sisi became Empress Elisabeth of Austria, wife of the Emperor Franz Joseph, but she never really liked court life in Vienna. She far preferred her family's home at Possenhofen on Starnbergersee, where she and her beloved cousin Ludwig spent their youthful summers, and where she returned frequently from Vienna. All over Bavaria you will find monuments and museums in Sisi's memory, rooms where she stayed and other mementoes. Sisi was assassinated in 1898, but in Bavaria you'd think everyone remembered her personally.

Of his varied collections, the paintings by the *Brücke* (Bridge) school artists are the most outstanding. ⓐ Am Hirschgarten 1, Bernried ⓣ (08158) 997 020 ⓦ www.buchheimmuseum.de ⓛ 10.00–18.00 Tues–Sun & holidays, Apr–Oct; 10.00–17.00 Tues–Sun & holidays, Nov–Mar ⓝ By boat from Starnberg and other lake points. Admission charge

Münterhaus

The story of Kandinsky in Murnau is Gabriele Münter's story, for although he was a great artist and philosopher, he was not the

⬥ *The Münterhaus in Murnau*

most constant lover. The house, which she bought for them at his request, contains copies of paintings and originals of prints by both of them (she was a noted artist, too). Wall paintings thought to be by her and furniture painted by Kandinsky are arranged just as they are shown in some of their paintings on display there. ⓐ Kottmüllerallee 6, Murnau ⓣ (08841) 628 880 ⓦ www.lenbachhaus.de ⓛ 14.00–17.00 Tues–Sun ⓝ Hourly rail service from Munich

Schlossmuseum

What the painters found here – the light, the scenery, the rural peace – and how they translated it in their painting, is explored in this excellent museum, where you learn exactly how the Blue Riders developed their style and philosophy. Extensive collections of local folk arts include *Hinterglasmalerei*, painting on glass. Its sharply defined fields of colour fascinated Münter and the others. ⓐ Schlossof 4–5, Murnau ⓣ (08841) 476 207 ⓦ www.schlossmuseum-murnau.de ⓛ 10.00–17.00 Tues–Sun (until 18.00 Sat & Sun July–Sept) ⓝ Hourly rail service from Munich. Admission charge

TAKING A BREAK

Uffing at the northern end of Staffelsee has a beer garden overlooking the lake. This is only one of dozens of places where you can enjoy a beer and a bite along with your lake views. The boats that ply most of the lakes all have attractive cafés and bars.

Forsthaus am See £ The large, tree-shaded beer garden overlooks

the lake. ❸ Am See 1, Possenhofen-Pocking ❶ (08157) 93010
Ⓦ www.forsthaus-am-see.de ⏱ 10.00–23.00

Gasthof zum Stern £ A traditional café with baked goods –
and a good choice for breakfast, too. The beer garden, shaded
by trees, is a great place for relaxation in summer. ❸ Dorfstr. 2,
Seehausen ❶ (08841) 3304 Ⓦ www.gasthof-stern.de
⏱ 08.00–01.00 (closed on Wed in winter)

AFTER DARK

RESTAURANTS
Griesbraeu zu Murnau £–££ Along with the genial restaurant
that serves regional dishes (including roast suckling pig), this
is a working brewery with a long brewing tradition. Take a tour
to see how they make the beers, which are 100 per cent natural.
❸ Obermarkt 37, Murnau ❶ (08841) 1422 Ⓦ www.griesbraeu.de
⏱ 11.30–14.00, 17.30–21.00 Tues, Wed, Fri–Sun

Seeblick ££ Traditional Bavarian dishes are served with more flair
and originality than elsewhere. Servings border on enormous,
and the desserts are outstanding. ❸ Tutzingerstr. 9, Bernried
❶ (08158) 2540 Ⓦ www.hotel-seeblick-bernried.de ⏱ 07.00–23.00

Hotel Schloss Berg ££–£££ The traditionally furnished dining
room is inviting, but elegant enough for a special evening out.
Look for excellent seasonal dishes, even an entire menu devoted
to asparagus in the spring. ❸ Seestr. 17, Berg ❶ (08151) 9630
Ⓦ www.hotelschlossberg.de ⏱ Lunch and dinner daily

Hoffmann's £££ Among the best in Bavaria, this Michelin-starred restaurant is elegant in both decor and cuisine, serving updated continental dishes in creative style. Heavenly desserts. ⓐ Ramsachstr. 8, Murnau ⓣ (08841) 4910 ⓦ www.alpenhof-murnau.com ⓛ Lunch and dinner daily

ACCOMMODATION

Starnberg has a wide range of places to stay, from 4-star hotels to cosy *pensions*. Hikers and climbers in the mountains can spend their nights along the high ridges or at the summit, staying in Alpine huts. Especially around Berchtesgaden, these huts are comfortable and offer spectacular sunrise and sunset views. ⓦ www.berchtesgadener-land.com

Hotel Seeblick £££ Within walking distance of the boat landing, in the centre of the attractive town, the hotel offers homely rooms, a swimming pool and a good restaurant. ⓐ Tutzingerstr. 9, Bernried ⓣ (08158) 2540 ⓦ www.hotel-seeblick-bernried.de

Hotel Kaiserin Elisabeth ££–£££ Sisi came here after she became Empress of Austria, along with her royal retinue of 50, and you can stay in her suite overlooking the park, with brass beds and carved *armoire*. The hotel is refreshingly unregal, enormously comfortable and warm, and well equipped. ⓐ Tutzingerstr. 2, Feldafing ⓣ (08157) 930 90 ⓦ www.kaiserin-elisabeth.de ⓝ S-Bahn: Feldafing

Alpenhof Murnau £££ This prestigious Relais & Châteaux property tops the list in Murnau for luxury lodgings and its

full-service spa. ⓐ Ramsachstr. 8, Murnau ⓣ (08841) 4910
ⓦ www.alpenhof-murnau.com

🔺 *Cruise boats ply the waters of the Starnbergersee*

Along the Danube

The Danube flows through Bavaria, north of Munich, on its way
from its source in the Black Forest to its mouth in the Black Sea.
Two of Bavaria's most interesting cites – Regensburg and Passau
– overlook its not-so-blue waters. Apart from the dramatic cliffs
of the Danube Gorge, the landscapes along the Danube are
gentle and rolling farmlands. A wide walking and cycling path
follows the entire river.

GETTING THERE

Regensburg is 90 minutes from Munich's Hauptbahnhof, with
hourly departures all day. Passau is about an hour by train from
Regensburg. Kelheim and Weltenburg are about an hour and
a half by car from Munich.

SIGHTS & ATTRACTIONS

Benerdiktinerabtei Weltenburg (Weltenburg Abbey)

As Bavaria's oldest monastery and the world's oldest monastery
brewery (records date back to 1050), Weltenburg would be worth
a stop just for a beer in its shady garden. But there is more: a good
restaurant, a beautiful setting on the Danube Gorge and a church
by the famous Asam brothers, who also built Munich's rococo
Asamkirche. The visitor centre explores the geology of the limestone
cliffs, which are part of the ancient seabed and appear to almost
push the 1,400-year-old monastery into the river. The church interior
is entirely baroque, but large enough to carry it off. The whole

impression is quite uplifting, right into the high dome which is filled with a host of clouds and cherubs. ⓐ Asamstrasse 32, Kelheim ❶ (09441) 5911 ⓦ www.urbanplus.com/weltenburg ❶ 10.00–18.00. Admission charge

Danube Gorge

The limestone cliffs drop so abruptly on both banks that the riverside path climbs over the mountain between Weltenburg and Kelheim – or you can make the scenic 30-minute trip through the gorge by boat. High above near Kelheim is Befreiungshalle (Liberation Hall), commemorating the wars against Napoleon in 1813–15. Boats run regularly between Kelheim and the riverside trail, about 400 m (437 yds) from Weltenburg Abbey.

DANUBE CRUISES

Passau and Regensburg are favourite stops for the Danube cruises operated by **Peter Deilmann** (ⓦ www.deilmann-cruises.com), **Viking River Cruises** (ⓦ www.vikingrivers.com) and others. These vary in length, some beginning with the Mainz–Danube canal and continuing all the way to the Black Sea. Others cover shorter stretches of the river, often from Passau to Budapest. For those who don't want a multi-night cruise, day cruises beginning in both Passau and Regensburg can be booked ahead or right at the river landings.
Passau ❶ (0851) 929 292 ⓦ www.donauschiffahrt.de
Regensburg ❶ (0941) 521 04 ⓦ www.schifffahrtklinger.de

The baroque Stephansdom in Passau

Boat tours ❷ Personenschiffahrt im Donau, Kelheim
❶ (09441) 5858 Ⓦ www.schiffahrt-kelheim.de ⏰ 10.00–17.00
May–Sept, less frequently Mar, Apr & Oct

Kelheim

At the other end of the boat ride is this pretty town with three
of the original tower gates of the medieval walls still standing.
You can see the old canal around the gorge, with locks and canal
houses, and the newer large canal that shunts shipping around
the gorge. Kelheim is small, but its old centre inside the walls is
charming, and there's an excellent brewery there.

Passau

Caught in the wedge of land between the Danube and the
River Inn, the city of Passau, with rivers on each side, is perfect
for exploring on foot, with stops in the cafés that line both the
riverbank and Ludwigstrasse.

The Rathaus, facing a broad riverside plaza, was rebuilt after
a 1662 fire. The exterior is striking, but don't miss the church-like
interior, with stained glass and murals of scenes from the
legends of the Nibelungs.

Stephansdom (St Stephen's Cathedral), the largest baroque
cathedral north of the Alps, sits on the hilltop at Domplatz.
Like the Rathaus, it was rebuilt after the 1662 fire, when Italian
architects and artists were brought in to build in the latest style.
The deeply carved designs of fruit, flowers and maize, as well as
the gold pulpit and stucco work on the arches, are their work. The
Dom contains the largest church organ in the world, connected
by 129 km (80 miles) of wiring, with 17,774 pipes. Organ concerts

held from May to October highlight modern music, including works by Muffet and Max Reiga. Special daily programmes are open to the public. ❶ (0851) 393 421 (for information on concerts) ❷ 06.30–19.00 summer; 06.30–18.00 winter; closed to visitors during church services and concerts

Regensburg

Among the best-preserved medieval cities in Germany, Regensburg is a university town with about 22,000 students. Most attractions are close together, including the beautiful Alte Kappel and St Peter's Cathedral, known for its stained-glass windows and the boys' choir that sings at mass each Sunday. In Domplatz opposite the cathedral, the Venetian façade is Haus Heuport, built by a minister of trade; its *piano nobile* is now a restaurant.

◆ *Regensburg is a favourite stop for Danube tours*

Wahlenstrasse, a fashionable street of homes built by medieval merchants returning from Italy, retains four of its original towers. Around the spacious Haidplatz is one of the city's oldest and most picturesque ensembles of buildings, including a medieval pilgrims' hostel. Past the Old Rathaus (with the excellent tourist information office) is a house on Goliathstrasse with a giant fresco of Goliath (look for the frog in the lower corner).

Stone Bridge, built in 1135–46, was until 1900 the only entrance to the city. At Neupfarrplatz, centre of the Old Ghetto, a memorial in the pavement was created from the foundations of the synagogue, and you can see Jewish cemetery stones in the surrounding buildings.

CULTURE

Document Neupfarrplatz

Beneath the pavement of the Old Ghetto, excavation unearthed the remains of Roman buildings, which have become an underground museum. Parts of the Roman military camp, Castra Regina, include the home of a high-ranking officer, and can be visited on scheduled tours with an English-speaking guide. ⓐ Neupfarrplatz (north side), tickets from Tabak Götz, Neupfarrplatz 3, Regensburg ⓣ (0941) 507 3442 ⓛ Tours: 14.30 Thur–Sat, Sept–June; 14.30 Thur–Mon, July & Aug. Admission charge

Glasmuseum Passau

Passau was at the end of the Glass Road, where 100 glassmakers once worked. Only five families still carry on the tradition, which is brilliantly represented in this private collection of glass from

the 1700s baroque and rococo, Empire, Biedermeier (1825–60) art nouveau, art deco and modern periods. The museum is much bigger than it looks, not a place for a half-hour run through. Also in the museum, which is in part of the Hotel Wilder Mann, is the suite where Empress Elisabeth stayed in 1862 and 1878, with original furniture and personal items including her gloves and shoes.
ⓐ Rathausplatz, Passau ① (0851) 35071 Ⓦ www.glasmuseum.de
🕐 13.00–17.00 daily. Admission charge

Oberhaus Museum

Built by Passau's prince-bishops, the massive castle high above the Danube and decorated with coats of arms is now a museum of local history. Exhibits illuminate the daily castle life, religious life and the lives of the lower classes on whose work the castle depended. Charles de Gaulle was held as a POW here during World War I. ⓐ Oberhaus 125, Passau ① (0851) 493 350
Ⓦ www.oberhausmuseum.de 🕐 09.00–17.00 Mon–Fri, 10.00–18.00 Sat, Sun & holidays, Apr–Oct. Ⓝ Oberhaus Museum bus every half hour 10.00–17.00 from quay 7 in front of Rathaus (tickets just opposite the tourist office). Admission charge

RETAIL THERAPY

Regensburg's old narrow streets offer good shopping, with antiques and crafts shops, fashion and household goods. Hollgasse is Passau's bohemian quarter, a narrow alley filled with shops and studios. Follow the painted paving stones to find one-off items in tiny shops such as Glasschnock Design Shintz, where the owner makes your jewellery to order while you watch.

Antikhaus Insam Lots of *Jugendstil*; the Tändlergasse shop has the world's largest selection of golf-related antiques – or so they claim. 🅐 Tändlergasse 11 and Landergasse 3, Regensburg 🅣 (0941) 51074 🅦 www.antikhaus-insam.de 🅛 10.00–18.00 Mon–Sat

Étagère Housewares, linens and gourmet foods inside the arched vaulting of a private chapel of one of the towered homes. 🅐 Wahlenstr. 16, Regensburg 16 🅣 (0941) 599 8298 🅦 www.etagere-regensburg.de 🅛 10.00–19.00 Mon–Fri, 10.00–18.00 Sat

Zanella Schmuckwerkstatt Beautiful handicrafts and art; look for her at Passau's Kristkindlmarkt (Christmas market), too. 🅐 Residenzplatz 1, Passau 🅣 (0851) 934 6041 🅦 www.julia-zanella.de 🅛 10.00–13.00, 14.00–18.00 Mon, Wed–Fri, 10.00–13.00 Sat

TAKING A BREAK

Klosterschenke Weltenburg £ Pause in your walk along the Danube for a beer and a *Brotzeit* (bread, cold cuts and cheeses), in the beer garden of the world's oldest monastery brewery. 🅐 Asamstr. 32, Weltenburg 🅣 (09441) 67570 🅦 www.klosterschenke-weltenburg.de 🅛 08.00–17.00 summer

Wurstkuchl £ A plate of sizzling homemade Regensburg *Bratwurst* and *Sauerkraut* from this riverside grill is a local tradition. Expect a queue any time, certainly to eat at the few tables in the atmospheric little dining room. 🅐 Thundorfer Str. 3, Regensburg 🅣 (0941) 466 210 🅦 http://wurstkuchl.de 🅛 09.00–19.00

AFTER DARK

Passau has five working breweries. None of them exports a drop; it is drunk right here, in litre steins. The record for how many of these a barmaid can carry full in two hands is 15. In Kelheim you'll find the oldest wheat beer brewery in Bavaria (which you can tour on Tuesdays).

RESTAURANTS

Weisses Brauhaus Kelheim £–££ A lovely beer garden where you can enjoy a Bavarian speciality, wheat beer, with dinner. ⓐ Emil-Ott-Str. 1–5, Kelheim ⓣ (09441) 3480 ⓦ www.weisses-brauhaus-kelheim.de ⓛ 09.00–00.00

Passauer Ratskeller ££ *Leberkasse*, in huge sizzling slabs, with big hot pretzels and spicy mustard is the typical (and hearty) lunch; dinner includes a wide range of local dishes. ⓐ Rathausplatz 2, Passau ⓣ (0851) 2630 ⓦ www.ratskeller-passau.de ⓛ 10.00–23.00 summer; 10.00–14.00, 17.00–22.00 winter

Haus Heuport ££–£££ Fast-serve lunches and dinners worth lingering over, with a view of the cathedral façade. ⓐ Domplatz, Regensburg ⓣ (0941) 599 9297 ⓦ www.heuport.de ⓛ 09.00–23.00 summer; 17.00–23.00 Mon–Fri, 09.00–23.00 Sat & Sun, winter

Heilig-Geist-Stiftschenke ££–£££ Tourists rarely find this popular downstairs den that dates from 1358. The schnitzel is outstanding, as is the roast pork. ⓐ Heiliggeiststr. 4, Passau ⓣ (0851) 2607 ⓦ www.stiftskeller-passau.de ⓛ 10.00–01.00 Thur–Tues

◆ *The Regensburger Dom (Regensburg Cathedral, see pages 119–20)*

Orphée ££–£££ Lamb provençal, coq au vin, veal with mushrooms and a number of vegetarian dishes share the menu at this smart, French-influenced dining room. ⓐ Untere Bachgasse 8, Regensburg ⓣ (0941) 52977 ⓦ www.hotel-orphee.de ⓛ 09.00–01.00

ACCOMMODATION

Rotel Inn £ Minuscule but cheap rooms, on the riverside bike path and popular with cyclists. ⓐ Donauufer, Passau ⓣ (0851) 95160 ⓦ www.rotel-inn.de

Hotel Orphée ££ Highly done-up rooms (you can browse photos to choose), with a nice café and a bodega. ⓐ Untere Bachgasse 8, Regensburg ⓣ (0941) 596 020 ⓦ www.hotel-orphee.de

Hotel Weisser Hase ££ Attractive modern rooms and good location just off Ludwigstrasse. ⓐ Heiliggeiststr. 1, Passau ⓣ (0851) 92110 ⓦ www.weisser-hase.de

Roter Hahn Hotel ££–£££ Located in the heart of the old town in a side alley, this family-run hotel with restaurant has stylish and clean rooms. ⓐ Rote Hahnengasse 10, Regensburg ⓣ (0941) 595 090 ⓦ www.roter-hahn.com

---

▶ *Munich airport information can answer most questions on arrival*

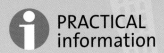

Directory

GETTING THERE

Munich's location in southern Germany makes it easily accessible from anywhere in Europe – or the world. Depending on where you begin, the options include air, rail, bus and car, or a combination of these.

By air

From the UK, you can get direct flights to Munich from Birmingham, Bristol, Edinburgh, London City, Stansted, Heathrow and Manchester airports. **easyJet** (ⓦ www.easyjet.com) serves Munich directly from both Stansted and Edinburgh, usually at serious bargain rates. **British Airways** (ⓦ www.britishairways.com) has regular flights direct to Munich from London and Bristol, occasionally at competitive rates. **Lufthansa** (ⓦ www.lufthansa.com), Germany's national airline, offers regular flights direct to Munich from both Heathrow and London City Airport. Flights from elsewhere in Europe are equally easy to find, since Munich is Germany's second largest airport.

Although there are fewer ready-made packages to Munich than to resort holiday havens, you can sometimes save by combining hotel and car hire with your airfare when booking flights. Especially when booking an entire package, it is wise to secure your trip with travel insurance, either through your tour operators or independently to protect your investment.

Many people are aware that air travel emits CO_2, which contributes to climate change. You may be interested in the possibility of lessening the environmental impact of your flight through the charity **Climate Care** (Ⓦ www.climatecare.org), which offsets your CO_2 by funding environmental projects around the world.

By train

Trains equipped with couchettes and sleepers take about 18 hours to Munich from either Calais or Ostend. Travellers from outside Europe who plan to use trains should investigate the various

⬤ *Bus tickets must be validated*

multi-day train passes on German railways and multi-country travel offered by **Rail Europe** (W www.raileurope.com). For travellers anywhere, Rail Europe offers a one-stop source of information, reservations and tickets, including Eurostar.

By bus

It's certainly not the fastest way, but it may well be the cheapest. **Eurolines** (T 08705 143 219 W www.eurolines.com) operates from London's Victoria Coach Station, taking around 19 hours.

By car

Germany's motorway (*Autobahn*) system is excellent, connecting all major cities within the country as well as the entry points from other European capitals.

Munich's city centre is an *Umweltzone* (Green Zone), and only low-emission cars with an *Umweltplakette* (Environment Sticker) are allowed to drive there. See page 51 for more details.

ENTRY FORMALITIES

Those arriving from other EU countries, the USA, Canada, Australia, New Zealand and several other countries need only a valid passport to stay in Germany for three months. Those from elsewhere should check with their nearest German embassy or consulate for current regulations. For information in English W www.auswaertiges-amt.de

EU citizens can bring goods for personal use when arriving from another EU country, but must observe the limits on tobacco

(800 cigarettes) and alcohol (10 litres of spirits over 22 per cent alcohol, 90 litres of wine). Limits for non-EU nationals are 200 cigarettes and one litre of spirits, two of wine.

MONEY

Germany uses the euro, and exchange can be made at the airport on arrival or at banks or any post office. Avoid carrying large amounts of cash, and hide what you must carry in several concealed pockets and security pouches. Traveller's cheques, accepted at banks, large hotels and by larger stores, are safer but difficult to cash elsewhere. If possible, bring at least one major credit card; VISA is the most commonly accepted. Most small hotels, *pension* and many small restaurants and shops do not accept cards. You're likely to have trouble cashing Eurocheques except in large banks.

Best for obtaining euros are credit or debit cards. Cashpoints offer the best exchange rates, and are found even in small towns. Banks are usually open 08.30–12.30 and 13.30–15.30 Monday–Friday. The bank at Central Station (Hauptbahnhof) is open daily 06.00–23.00. It's best to have enough euros to last over weekends, when banks close and ATMs may be out of money or out of order. Try to arrive with euros, especially at a weekend.

HEALTH, SAFETY & CRIME

Drinking water is safe in Munich, as is food, although it is wise to carry your favourite medication for an upset stomach, since travellers anywhere are more likely to eat and drink things their systems are unaccustomed to.

European Union members are entitled to free or reduced-cost emergency medical treatment in Germany on presentation of a valid European Health Insurance Card (EHIC). You will still be charged a practice fee of €10 if you visit a doctor or dentist. If you are hospitalised, you will be charged €10 a day for a maximum of 28 days.

Apply for the EHIC online at ⓦ www.nhs.uk/Healthcareabroad and allow at least a week to receive it.

It is important to remember that the EHIC is not an alternative to travel insurance and will not cover aspects such as repatriation back to your home country.

Non-EU residents should carry travel health insurance if their own coverage does not cover reimbursement, and should also consider emergency medical repatriation insurance. Emergency treatment at hospitals is free to everyone.

The **US consulate** (ⓦ http://munich.usconsulate.gov) maintains a list of medical suppliers who are fluent in English.

Munich is a relatively safe city with a crime rate lower than any other major German city, although in any city you should be alert and aware of your surroundings, avoiding deserted streets, especially at night.

For police and medical emergency numbers and addresses, see Emergencies, pages 138–9.

OPENING HOURS

Shops in central Munich are usually open Monday to Friday from 09.00–20.00 and on Saturday from 09.00–16.00. In smaller towns and in outer neighbourhoods, shops may open Monday to Friday between 08.00 and 09.00, closing at about

18.00. An hour closing at lunchtime is not unusual. Saturday opening is usually only until 12.00 or 13.00. Supermarkets tend to keep longer hours. Most shops, except at Munich's airport, are closed on Sunday.

TOILETS

Public toilets (*Toiletten*) are plentiful, well signposted and unfailingly clean. Look for signs indicating *Damen* (women) and *Herren* (men). Be prepared with small coins either for a coin-operated door or for the person who services the facilities.

CHILDREN

Bavarians love children, and often travel with their own, so facilities for youngsters are plentiful. Swings and play areas are common in parks and museums often have sections for children, or at least some interactive exhibits. Highchairs and booster seats are available in all but the smartest restaurants and discounted or free admission is offered at attractions. Hotels can usually provide cots, with advance notice, and you will rarely be charged for a child staying in a room with adults. Special infant needs, such as baby food and nappies, are available in supermarkets, but for a shorter stay it is easier to bring familiar brands from home.

Although not every place is suitable for all ages, kids like watching the moving figures in the Glockenspiel (small children will certainly need a boost onto someone's shoulders to see) and perhaps a trip up the Rathaus tower or one of the others nearby – Frauenkirche or Peterskirche – to look down on the city. The other most child-friendly sights are the **Spielzeugmuseum** (Toy Museum

ⓐ Marienplatz 15 ⓣ (049) 8929 4001 ⓦ www.spielzeugmuseum-
muenchen.de), the puppets in the Stadtmuseum (see page 69),
and the endless variety of interactive exhibits at the Deutsches
Museum (see page 82). Older children will like Nymphenburg
Palace (see page 94) and the royal coaches in the adjoining stables.

Castles are a good bet, and you can be sure they will love
Neuschwanstein with its fairy-tale towers. And a trip up the
Zugspitze on the train and cable car is exciting for any age.

Boat rides on the Danube or one of the lakes are always
a good bet; Starnbergersee boats have play areas for children,
including a tube slide on the top deck. In any town, but especially
those on the lakes, look for kiddie playgrounds, with slides and
climbing frames, swings and other toys. These also provide
a place to find playmates (who don't care if they don't speak
the same language). Beer gardens will nearly always have
playgrounds to occupy small fry while parents relax with a beer.

Festivals always have children's activities and are colourful,
lively occasions with lively Bavarian music. Having a child with
you is your best ticket to becoming part of the festivities instead
of a spectator.

COMMUNICATIONS
Internet
Internet access is increasingly available, both in hotels and
internet points and cafés around the city. Most 4- and 5-star
hotels have in-room points, and others will probably allow you
to plug into their phone systems. The tourist information office
and kiosks can provide lists of internet cafés and public access
points such as libraries.

TELEPHONING GERMANY

To call Munich from outside Germany, dial 0049 for Germany, then the number, dropping the first 'o'.

TELEPHONING ABROAD

To make an international call, dial 00, then the country code (UK = 44, Ireland = 353, US and Canada = 1, Australia = 61, New Zealand = 64) and number, omitting the initial zero in UK numbers.

Post

The main post office in each town is usually near the main railway station, and provides currency exchange as well as selling stamps. You can also buy stamps at news stands.

ELECTRICITY

Electrical appliances used in the UK will work in Germany, but those from the US and Canada will need an adaptor to convert from 110 V to 220 V AC. Plugs are two pin and round-pronged.

DISABLED TRAVELLERS

Germany is ahead of the curve on access for visitors with disabilities, which will be available in all recently built buildings. Access to historic properties is patchy, but lifts are often available. If in doubt, it is best to call ahead. Most tourist offices have a list of accessible sights, hotels and restaurants. For information on assistance at Munich airport contact ☎ (089) 9756 3333 ✉ mail@md-medicus.net. For current information before leaving home, contact **RADAR** (📧 12 City Forum, 250 City Road, London EC1V 8AF 📞 020 7250 3222 🌐 www.radar.org.uk)

TOURIST INFORMATION

Munich Tourist Information 📞 (089) 2339 6500 🌐 www.muenchen-tourist.de 🕐 Telephone information: 08.00–19.00 Mon–Fri, 09.00–17.00 Sat

Tourist Info Hauptbahnhof 📧 Hauptbahnhof (main railway station) 🕐 09.30–20.30 Mon–Sat, 10.00–18.00 Sun

Tourist Info Marienplatz 📧 Neues Rathaus, Marienplatz 🕐 10.00–20.00 Mon–Fri, 10.00–16.00 Sat

Murnau Tourist Office 📧 Kohlgruberstr. 1, Murnau 📞 (08841) 61410 🌐 www.theblueland.de 🕐 09.00–12.00, 14.00–17.00 Mon–Fri, 10.00–12.00 Sat

Passau Tourist Information 📧 Rathausplatz, Passau 📞 (0851) 955 980 🕐 08.30–17.00 Mon–Thur, 08.30–16.00 Fri

Regensburg Tourist Information 📧 Altes Rathaus, Rathausplatz 4, Regensburg 📞 (0941) 507 4410 🌐 www.regensburg.de 🕐 09.00–18.00 Mon–Fri, 09.00–16.00 Sat, 09.30–16.00 Sun (closes 14.30 in winter)

Starnberger-Funf-Seen-Land Tourismusverband
📧 Wittelsbacherstr. 2C, Starnberg 📞 (08151) 906 00 🌐 www.sta5.de 🕐 08.00–18.00 Mon–Fri (also 09.00–17.00 Sat in summer)

Useful websites

🌐 www.muenchen-tourist.de

🌐 www.theblueland.de (Murnau and Staffelsee region)

🌐 www.sta5.de (Starnberg and Starnbergersee area)

🌐 www.regensburg.de

Ⓦ www.tourismus.passau.de

Ⓦ www.tourismus-landkreis-kelheim.de (Kelheim–Danube Gorge)

German National Tourist Offices overseas

Ⓐ 122 E 42nd St 2000, New York, NY 10168, USA Ⓣ 212 661 7200

Ⓦ www.cometogermany.com

Ⓐ 480 University Avenue, Suite 1410, Toronto, Ontario M5G 1V2, Canada Ⓣ 416 968 1685 Ⓦ www.cometogermany.com

Ⓐ PO Box 2695, London W1A 3TN, UK Ⓣ 020 7317 0908

Ⓦ www.germany-tourism.co.uk

Ⓐ PO Box A980, Sydney South, NSW 1236, Australia

Ⓣ 02 8296 0488

◉ Get the most from your stay in Munich

Emergencies

EMERGENCY NUMBERS
Police ☏ 110
Ambulance ☏ 112
Fire ☏ 112
Medical assistance ☏ 551 771

MEDICAL SERVICES
General Hospital Munich (Klinikum Schwabing)
Munich's largest hospital, with English-speaking staff.
ⓐ Kölner Platz 1 ☏ (089) 306 80 Ⓦ www.kms.mhn.de

POLICE
Central police station (*Polizei*) ⓐ Arnulfstr. (beside the
Hauptbahnhof) ☏ (089) 578 38801 ⓛ 24 hours

Lost property ⓐ Oetztalerstr. 17 ☏ (089) 233 00
For items lost on trains, see the Fundstelle der Bundesbahn
opposite platform 26 at the Hauptbahnhof. ☏ (089) 1308 6664

EMBASSIES & CONSULATES
British Consulate General ⓐ Burkleinstr. 10, Munich
☏ (089) 211 090 Ⓦ http://ukingermany.fco.gov.uk
American Consulate General ⓐ Königinstr. 5, Munich
☏ (089) 288 880 Ⓦ http://munich.usconsulate.gov
Australian Embassy ⓐ Wallstr. 76-79, 10179 Berlin
☏ (030) 700 129 129 Ⓦ www.germany.embassy.gov.au

EMERGENCY PHRASES

Help!	**Fire!**	**Stop!**
Hilfe!	Feuer!	Halt!
Heelfe!	*Foyer!*	*Halt!*

Please call an ambulance/a doctor/the police/ the fire service!
Rufen Sie bitte einen Krankenwagen/einen Arzt/ die Polizei/die Feuerwehr!
Roofen zee bitter inen krankenvaagen/inen artst/ dee politsye/dee foyervair!

Canadian Consulate ⓐ Tal 29, Munich ⓣ (089) 2199 570
ⓦ www.international.gc.ca
Consulate of Ireland ⓐ Denningerstr. 15, Munich
ⓣ (089) 2080 5990
South African Consul General ⓐ Sendlinger-Tor-Platz 5, Munich
ⓣ (089) 231 1630 ⓦ www.suedafrika.org

INDEX

Editorial/project management: Lisa Plumridge
Copy editor: Paul Hines
Layout/DTP: Alison Rayner

The publishers would like to thank the following individuals
and organisations for providing their copyright photographs
for this book: Deutsches Museum Munich Tourist Office, page 83;
Flughafen Munich GmbH, page 127; Pablo Lucas dos Anjos, page 21;
Münchner Verkehrs- und Tarifverbund GmbH, page 129; Pictures
Colour Library, pages 15, 23, 42–3, 50 & 97; C Reiter/Munich Tourist
Office, page 7; Johannes Seyerlein/Staatstheater am Gärtnerplatz,
page 34; Tollwood GmbH, page 32; World Pictures, pages 1, 17,
59 & 91; Stillman Rogers, all others.

Send your thoughts to
books@thomascook.com

- Found a great bar, club, shop or must-see sight that we don't feature?
- Like to tip us off about any information that needs a little updating?
- Want to tell us what you love about this handy little guidebook and
  more importantly how we can make it even handier?

Then here's your chance to tell all! Send us ideas, discoveries and
recommendations today and then look out for your valuable input
in the next edition of this title.

Email the above address (stating the title) or write to:
CitySpots Series Editor, Thomas Cook Publishing, PO Box 227,
Coningsby Road, Peterborough PE3 8SB, UK.